This book is to be returned on or before the date above.
It may be borrowed for a further period if not in demand.

Essex County Council

D1335689

30130 142473403

Published in 2006 by Murdoch Books Pty Limited.
www.murdochbooks.com.au

Murdoch Books Australia
Pier 8/9, 23 Hickson Road
Millers Point NSW 2000
Phone: + 61 (0) 2 8220 2000
Fax: + 61 (0) 2 8220 2558

Murdoch Books UK Limited
Erico House, 6th Floor North
93–99 Upper Richmond Road
Putney, London SW15 2TG
Phone: + 44 (0) 20 8785 5995
Fax: + 44 (0) 20 8785 5985

Chief Executive: Juliet Rogers
Publishing Director: Kay Scarlett

Design Manager: Vivien Valk
Concept & Art Direction: Sarah Odgers
Design: Jacqueline Duncan
Project Manager: Paul McNally
Editor: Gordana Trifunovic
Photographer: Jared Fowler
Stylist: Cherise Koch
Food preparation: Alan Wilson
Introduction text: Leanne Kitchen
Recipes developed by the Murdoch Books Test Kitchen
Production: Monika Paratore

National Library of Australia Cataloguing-in-Publication Data
Celebration. Includes index.
ISBN 978 1 74045 961 7. ISBN 1 74045 961 X.
1. Christmas cookery (Series: Kitchen Classics; 1). 641.5686

Printed by 1010 Printing International Ltd. in 2006. PRINTED IN CHINA.

IMPORTANT: Those who might be at risk from the effects of salmonella poisoning (the elderly, pregnant women, young children and those suffering from immune deficiency diseases) should consult their doctor with any concerns about eating raw eggs.

CONVERSION GUIDE: You may find cooking times vary depending on the oven you are using. For fan-forced ovens, as a general rule, set the oven temperature to 20°C (35°F) lower than indicated in the recipe. We have used 20 ml (4 teaspoon) tablespoon measures. If you are using a 15 ml (3 teaspoon) tablespoon, for most recipes the difference will not be noticeable. However, for recipes using baking powder, gelatine, bicarbonate of soda (baking soda), small amounts of flour, add an extra teaspoon for each tablespoon specified.

celebration

THE CHRISTMAS RECIPES
YOU MUST HAVE

MURDOCH BOOKS

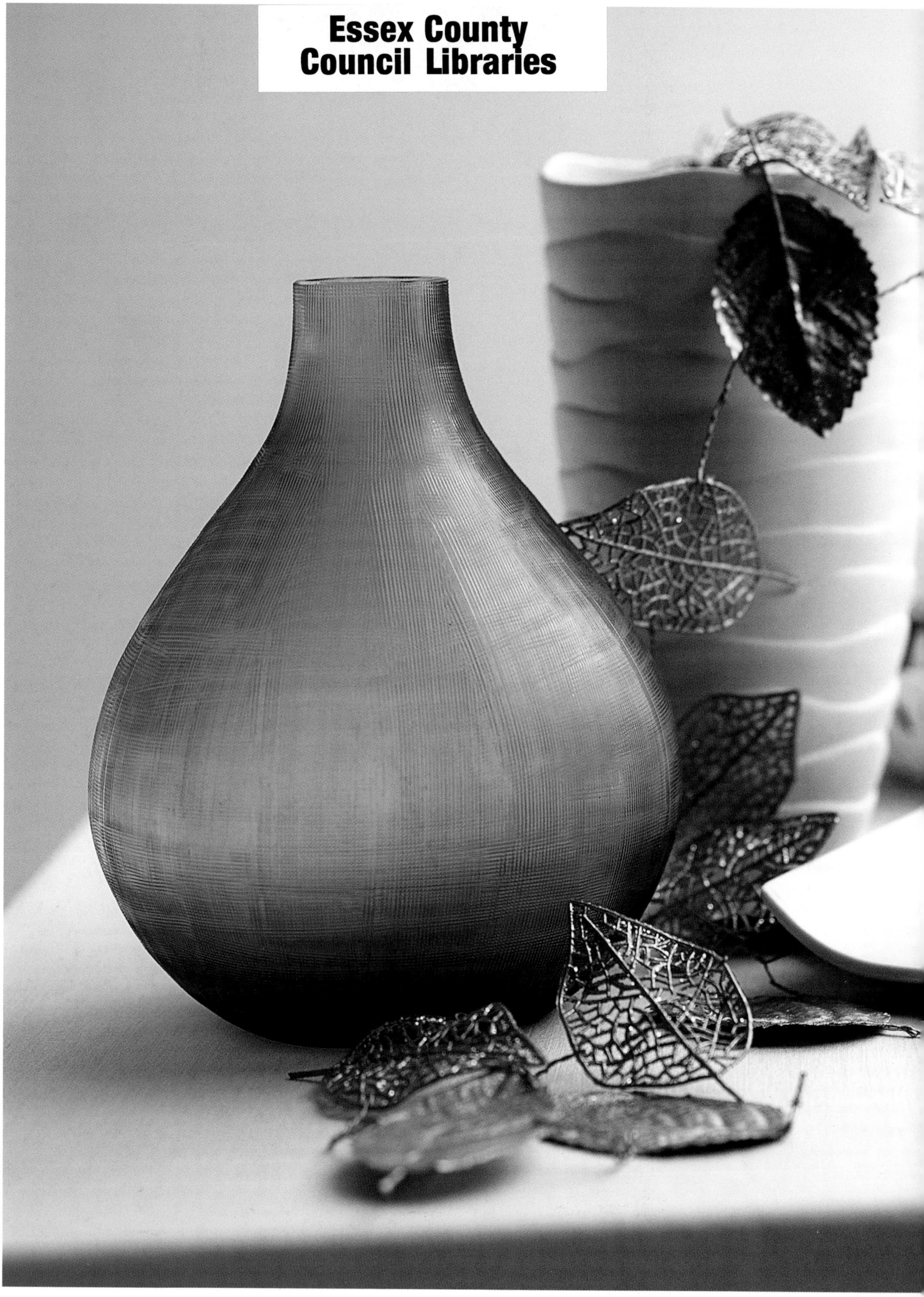

CONTENTS

ALL THE TRIMMINGS

'In my experience' claimed the legendary British food writer Jane Grigson, '... clever food is not appreciated at Christmas. It makes the little ones cry and the old ones nervous.'

It's true that at this most anticipated time of the year, with all the attendant fuss, festivities and, most importantly, feasting, food is uppermost on everyone's minds and we count on recipes that yield memorable results yet are not overly tricky. For many of us, Christmas is the time to rustle up time-honoured favourites — devils on horseback, roast, stuffed turkey, a sumptuous glazed ham, some decadent eggnog, and a devastatingly rich steamed plum pudding, for example. Such fare is entirely welcome for more formal, sit-down affairs in cooler climates — even in Southern Hemisphere households, where December spells the height of summer, this traditional approach has many fans. A looser style of Christmas entertaining is now considered equally appropriate however, especially with many busy cooks succumbing to 'time poverty'. Sensationally simple barbecued meats, teamed with an array of vibrant salads or hot vegetable dishes, are utterly essential, as are platters overflowing with grilled seafood, offered buffet-style alongside an arrangement of accompaniments. Whichever catering style one opts for though, Christmas entertaining demands the serving of all those lovely extras that mark this celebration as singular. What would Christmas be without fruity cheese logs, jugs of sparkling punch, plus offerings of sweet, mince tarts, cinnamon stars and buttery shortbread? Containing recipes for every inclination and preference, *Celebration* is the book every Christmas cook has been waiting for. With its wealth of dependable, delicious recipes, there is inspiration galore here for every style of festive entertaining imaginable.

STARTERS

SMOKED SALMON TARTLETS

250 g (9 oz) cream cheese,
at room temperature
1½ tablespoons wholegrain mustard
2 teaspoons dijon mustard
2 tablespoons lemon juice
2 tablespoons chopped dill
6 sheets ready-rolled puff pastry
300 g (10½ oz) smoked salmon, cut into
thin strips
2 tablespoons bottled capers, drained
dill sprigs, to garnish

MAKES 24

Preheat the oven to 210°C (415°F/Gas 6–7). Line two large baking trays with baking paper. Mix the cream cheese, mustards, lemon juice and dill in a bowl, then cover and refrigerate.

Cut four 9.5 cm (3¾ inch) rounds from each sheet of puff pastry, using a fluted cutter, and place on the baking trays. Prick the pastries all over. Cover and refrigerate for 10 minutes.

Bake the pastries in batches for 7 minutes, then remove from the oven and use a spoon to flatten the centre of each pastry. Return to the oven and bake for a further 5 minutes, or until the pastry is golden. Allow to cool.

Spread some of the cream cheese mixture over each pastry round, leaving a 1 cm (½ inch) border. Arrange the salmon over the top. Decorate with a few capers and a sprig of dill. Serve immediately.

PREPARATION TIME: 30 MINUTES +   COOKING TIME: 30 MINUTES

PUFF PASTRY TWISTS

2 sheets ready-rolled puff pastry, thawed
1 egg, lightly beaten
80 g (2¾ oz/½ cup) sesame seeds,
poppy seeds or caraway seeds

MAKES 96

Preheat the oven to 200°C (400°F/Gas 6). Lightly grease two baking trays. Brush the pastry with the egg and sprinkle with the sesame seeds.

Cut the pastry in half crossways and then into 1 cm (½ inch) wide strips. Twist the strips and place on the greased baking trays. Bake for about 10 minutes, or until golden brown.

PREPARATION TIME: 10 MINUTES   COOKING TIME: 10 MINUTES PER BATCH

NOTE: Store in an airtight container for up to 1 week. Refresh in a 180°C (350°F/Gas 4) oven for 2–3 minutes, then allow to cool.

SPINACH DIP

250 g (9 oz) frozen chopped spinach
300 g (10½ oz) ricotta cheese
185 g (6½ oz/¾ cup) sour cream
30 g (1 oz) packet spring vegetable soup mix
4 spring onions (scallions), finely chopped

SERVES 6–8

Thaw the spinach and squeeze out the liquid using your hands.

Process the spinach, ricotta, sour cream, soup mix and spring onion in a food processor until smooth. Cover and refrigerate for 2–3 hours.

Serve with crisp lavash bread, biscuits or assorted crisp vegetables such as blanched snow peas (mangetout), cauliflower and carrots.

PREPARATION TIME: 10 MINUTES +   COOKING TIME: NIL

NOTE: This dip can be made up to 1 week in advance.

CHICKEN LIVER AND GRAND MARNIER PÂTÉ

750 g (1 lb 10 oz) chicken livers,
well trimmed
250 ml (9 fl oz/1 cup) milk
200 g (7 oz) butter, softened
4 spring onions (scallions), finely chopped
1 tablespoon Grand Marnier
1 tablespoon frozen orange juice
concentrate, thawed
1/2 orange, very thinly sliced

JELLIED LAYER
1 tablespoon orange juice concentrate
1 tablespoon Grand Marnier
315 ml (10 3/4 fl oz/1 1/4 cups) canned
chicken consommé, undiluted
2 1/2 teaspoons powdered gelatine

SERVES 8

Put the chicken livers in a bowl, add the milk and stir to combine. Cover and refrigerate for 1 hour. Drain the livers and discard the milk. Rinse in cold water, drain and pat dry with paper towels.

Melt a third of the butter in a frying pan, add the spring onion and cook for 2–3 minutes, or until tender, but not brown. Add the livers and cook, stirring, over medium heat for 4–5 minutes, or until just cooked. Remove from the heat and cool a little.

Transfer the livers to a food processor and process until very smooth. Chop the remaining butter, add to the processor with the Grand Marnier and orange juice concentrate and process until creamy. Season, to taste, with salt and freshly ground black pepper. Transfer to a 1.25 litre (44 fl oz) serving dish, cover the surface with plastic wrap and chill for 1 1/2 hours, or until firm.

For the jellied layer, whisk together the orange juice concentrate, Grand Marnier and 125 ml (4 fl oz/1/2 cup) of the consommé in a jug. Sprinkle the gelatine over the liquid in an even layer and leave until the gelatine is spongy — do not stir. Heat the remaining consommé in a pan, remove from the heat and add the gelatine mixture. Stir to dissolve the gelatine, then leave to cool and thicken to the consistency of uncooked egg white, but not set.

Press the orange slices lightly into the surface of the pâté and spoon the thickened jelly evenly over the top. Refrigerate until set. Serve at room temperature with toast or crackers.

PREPARATION TIME: 20 MINUTES +   COOKING TIME: 10 MINUTES

NOTE: Grand Marnier is a cognac-based liqueur with an orange flavour.

Chicken liver and Grand Marnier pâté

MINI EGGS FLORENTINE

8 slices white bread
1-2 tablespoons olive oil
12 quail eggs
2 teaspoons lemon juice
85 g (3 oz) butter, melted, cooled
2 teaspoons finely chopped basil
20 g (3/4 oz) butter, extra
50 g (1 3/4 oz) baby English spinach leaves

MAKES 24

Preheat the oven to 180°C (350°F/Gas 4). Cut 24 rounds from the bread with a 4 cm (1 1/2 inch) cutter. Brush both sides of the rounds with the olive oil and bake for 10-15 minutes, or until golden brown.

Add the quail eggs to a small saucepan of cold water. Bring to the boil, stirring gently (to centre the yolk) and simmer for 4 minutes. Drain, then soak in cold water until cool. Peel, then cut in half, remove the yolks and reserve the whites.

Process the quail egg yolks and lemon juice together in a food processor for 10 seconds. With the motor running, add the cooled melted butter in a thin stream. Add the chopped basil and process until combined.

Melt the extra butter in a saucepan, add the spinach leaves and toss until just wilted. Place a little on each bread round, top each with half a quail egg white and fill the cavity with the basil mixture.

PREPARATION TIME: 20 MINUTES   COOKING TIME: 25 MINUTES

HERB CHEESE LOG

500 g (1 lb 2 oz) cream cheese, at room temperature
1 tablespoon lemon juice
1 garlic clove, crushed
2 teaspoons chopped thyme
2 teaspoons chopped tarragon
1 tablespoon chopped flat-leaf (Italian) parsley
50 g (1 3/4 oz/1 cup) snipped chives

SERVES 12

Beat the cream cheese in a large bowl with electric beaters until soft and creamy. Mix in the lemon juice and garlic. In a separate bowl, combine the thyme, tarragon and parsley.

Line a 20 x 30 cm (8 x 12 inch) shallow tin with foil. Spread the chives over the base, then dollop the cream cheese over the chives. Using a palette knife, gently join the dollops, spreading the mixture and pushing it into any gaps. Sprinkle the herbs over the cheese. Lift the foil from the tin and place on a work surface. Roll into a log, starting from the longest edge, then cover and place on a baking tray.

Refrigerate for at least 3 hours, or overnight. Serve with crackers.

PREPARATION TIME: 25 MINUTES +   COOKING TIME: NIL

PESTO PALMIERS

1 large handful basil
1 garlic clove, crushed
25 g (1 oz) grated parmesan cheese
1 tablespoon pine nuts, toasted
2 tablespoons olive oil
4 sheets ready-rolled puff pastry, thawed

MAKES 60

Preheat the oven to 220°C (425°F/Gas 7). Roughly chop the basil in a food processor with the garlic, parmesan and pine nuts. With the motor running, gradually add the oil in a thin stream and process until smooth.

Spread each pastry sheet with a quarter of the basil mixture. Roll up one side until you reach the middle then, repeat with the other side. Place on a baking tray. Repeat with the remaining pastry and basil mixture. Freeze for 30 minutes.

Slice each roll into 1.5 cm (^{5}/$_8$ inch) slices. Curl each slice into a semi-circle and place on a lightly greased baking tray. Allow room for the palmiers to expand during cooking. Bake in batches for 15–20 minutes, or until golden brown.

PREPARATION TIME: 20 MINUTES   COOKING TIME: 15 MINUTES PER BATCH

NOTE: Other savoury variations include spreading with a prepared tapenade paste made with olives, capers, anchovies, oil and garlic, or with tahini. Another simple version is to sprinkle just the grated parmesan between the pastry layers.

SPICY NUTS

2 tablespoons olive oil
½ teaspoon ground cumin
½ teaspoon ground coriander
½ teaspoon garlic powder
¼ teaspoon chilli powder
¼ teaspoon ground ginger
¼ teaspoon ground cinnamon
65 g (2¼ oz/⅔ cup) pecans
100 g (3½ oz/⅔ cup) raw cashew nuts
240 g (8½ oz/1½ cups) raw almonds

SERVES 6

Preheat the oven to 150°C (300°F/Gas 2). Heat the oil over low heat in a large frying pan and stir in the spices for 2 minutes, or until fragrant. Remove from the heat, add the nuts and stir with a wooden spoon until the nuts are well coated. Spread over a baking tray and bake for 15 minutes, or until golden. Sprinkle with salt and cool.

PREPARATION TIME: 10 MINUTES   COOKING TIME: 20 MINUTES

CHEESE SNACKS

125 g (4½ oz/1 cup) plain
(all-purpose) flour
pinch of cayenne pepper
pinch of powdered mustard
80 g (2¾ oz) butter, chopped
125 g (4½ oz) cheddar cheese,
finely grated
1 egg yolk
1-2 teaspoons lemon juice
paprika, for dusting

MAKES ABOUT 30

Preheat the oven to 210°C (415°F/Gas 6-7). Lightly grease two baking trays.

Sift the flour, cayenne pepper and mustard into a large bowl. Rub in the butter with your fingertips until the mixture resembles fine breadcrumbs. Stir in the cheese. Make a well in the centre, add the egg yolk and lemon juice and mix with a flat-bladed knife, using a cutting action, until the mixture comes together in beads. Gently gather the dough together and lift out onto a lightly floured work surface. Gather into a ball, wrap in plastic wrap and refrigerate for 20 minutes.

Roll out the pastry on a lightly floured surface to about 5 mm (¼ inch) thick. Cut out biscuits with a floured Christmas-tree cutter. Gather the leftover dough together and re-roll. Place on the trays and bake for 6-8 minutes, or until golden brown. Lightly dust with paprika.

PREPARATION TIME: 25 MINUTES +   COOKING TIME: 8 MINUTES

MUSHROOMS WITH TWO SAUCES

750 g (1 lb 10 oz) button mushrooms
40 g (1½ oz/⅓ cup) plain
(all-purpose) flour
100 g (3½ oz/1 cup) dry breadcrumbs
3 eggs
olive oil, for deep-frying

SAUCES
1 small red capsicum (pepper)
2 egg yolks
1 teaspoon dijon mustard
1 tablespoon lemon juice
250 ml (9 fl oz/1 cup) olive oil
1 small garlic clove, crushed
2 tablespoons plain yoghurt
2 teaspoons finely chopped flat-leaf
(Italian) parsley

SERVES 8

Wipe the mushrooms with paper towels and remove the stems. Measure the flour into a large plastic bag and the breadcrumbs into a separate bag. Lightly beat the eggs in a bowl.

Put the mushrooms in with the flour and shake until evenly coated. Shake off any excess flour, then dip half the mushrooms in egg to coat well. Transfer to the bag with the breadcrumbs and shake to cover thoroughly. Place on a tray covered with baking paper. Repeat with the remaining mushrooms, then refrigerate for 1 hour.

Cut the capsicum into large flattish pieces, discarding the membranes and seeds. Cook, skin-side-up, under a hot grill (broiler) until the skin blackens and blisters. Cool in a plastic bag, then peel. Process in a food processor or blender to a smooth paste.

Place the egg yolks, mustard and half the lemon juice in a bowl. Beat together for 1 minute using electric beaters. Add the oil, a teaspoon at a time, beating constantly until thick and creamy. Continue beating until all the oil is added, then add the remaining lemon juice. Divide the mayonnaise between two bowls. Into one, stir the garlic, yoghurt and parsley and into the other, the red capsicum mixture.

Fill a heavy-based saucepan one-third full of oil and heat the oil to 180°C (350°F), or until a cube of bread dropped into the oil browns in 15 seconds. Gently lower batches of the mushrooms into the oil and cook for 1–2 minutes, or until golden brown. Remove with a slotted spoon and drain on paper towels.

To serve, arrange the mushrooms on serving plates and fill each mushroom with either of the sauces. If you prefer, you can spoon a little of each sauce into each mushroom.

PREPARATION TIME: 30 MINUTES +   COOKING TIME: 10 MINUTES

NOTE: Cook the mushrooms just before serving. The sauces can be made up to 1 day ahead and refrigerated, covered.

TOMATO AND BASIL CROUSTADES

1 day-old unsliced white bread loaf

3 tablespoons olive oil

2 garlic cloves, crushed

3 tomatoes, diced

250 g (9 oz) bocconcini (fresh baby mozzarella cheese), cut into small chunks

1 tablespoon tiny capers, rinsed and dried

1 tablespoon extra virgin olive oil

2 teaspoons balsamic vinegar

4 tablespoons shredded basil

SERVES 4

Preheat the oven to 180°C (350°F/Gas 4). Remove the crusts from the bread and cut the loaf into four even pieces. Using a small serrated knife, cut a square from the centre of each cube of bread, leaving a border of about 1.5 cm (⅝ inch) on each side. You should be left with four 'boxes'. Combine the oil and garlic and brush all over the croustades. Place them on a baking tray and bake for about 20 minutes, or until golden and crisp. Check them occasionally to make sure they don't burn.

Meanwhile, combine the tomato and bocconcini with the tiny capers in a bowl.

In a bowl, stir together the oil and balsamic vinegar, then gently toss with the tomato mixture. Season with salt and freshly ground black pepper, then stir in the basil. Spoon into the croustades, allowing any excess to tumble over the sides.

PREPARATION TIME: 30 MINUTES   COOKING TIME: 20 MINUTES

SMOKED TROUT DIP

250 g (9 oz) smoked rainbow trout

1½ teaspoons olive oil

125 ml (4 fl oz/½ cup) pouring (whipping) cream

1 tablespoon lemon juice

pinch of cayenne pepper

SERVES 4–6

Remove the skin and bones from the smoked trout. Put the flesh in a food processor or blender with the olive oil, 2 teaspoons of the cream and the lemon juice. Blend to a thick paste, then slowly add the remaining cream until well mixed. Season, to taste, with salt and the cayenne pepper. Serve with grissini or water crackers and baby radishes or other vegetables, for dipping.

PREPARATION TIME: 25 MINUTES   COOKING TIME: NIL

NOTE: This dip can be made a few days ahead and kept, covered, in the refrigerator.

CHEESE FRUIT LOG

35 g (1¼ oz/¼ cup) shelled pistachio nuts
250 g (9 oz) cream cheese,
at room temperature
50 g (1¾ oz) dried apricots,
finely chopped
3 spring onions (scallions), finely chopped
45 g (1½ oz/¼ cup) sun-dried tomatoes,
drained, finely chopped
3 tablespoons finely chopped flat-leaf
(Italian) parsley

SERVES 6

Preheat the oven to 200°C (400°F/Gas 6). Bake the pistachio nuts on a lined baking tray for 5 minutes, or until golden brown. Cool, then finely chop.

Beat the cream cheese in a bowl until smooth. Fold in the dried apricot, spring onion and sun-dried tomato, and some freshly ground black pepper, to taste.

Sprinkle the combined pistachio nuts and parsley over a sheet of baking paper, shaping into a 20 cm x 6 cm (8 x 2½ inch) rectangle. Form the mixture into a 20 cm (8 inch) log and roll in the nut mixture. Wrap in plastic and refrigerate for 2–3 hours, or until firm. Serve with plain savoury biscuits.

PREPARATION TIME: 15 MINUTES +   COOKING TIME: 5 MINUTES

GRISSINI WRAPPED IN SMOKED SALMON

125 g (4½ oz) cream cheese,
at room temperature
1-2 tablespoons chopped dill
¼ teaspoon finely grated lemon zest
24 ready-made grissini
8-10 slices smoked salmon, cut into
thin strips

MAKES 24

Mix the cream cheese, fresh dill and lemon zest in a bowl until the dill is well distributed. Season, to taste, with salt. Spread some of the cream cheese mixture onto three-quarters of each length of grissini. Wrap the salmon around the stick, over the cheese, securing it with more cheese. Repeat with the remaining grissini.

PREPARATION TIME: 20 MINUTES   COOKING TIME: NIL

NOTE: Prepare these grissini close to serving (up to about 30 minutes before) as the biscuits will start to soften once the cheese is spread on them.

MUSHROOM PÂTÉ

40 g (1½ oz) butter
1 tablespoon oil
400 g (14 oz) flat mushrooms, chopped
2 garlic cloves, crushed
3 spring onions (scallions), chopped
1 tablespoon lemon juice
100 g (3½ oz) ricotta cheese
100 g (3½ oz) cream cheese,
at room temperature
2 tablespoons chopped coriander
(cilantro) leaves

SERVES 8-10

Heat the butter and oil in a large frying pan over medium heat. Add the mushrooms and garlic. Cook for 5 minutes, or until the mushrooms have softened and the mushroom liquid has evaporated. Stir in the spring onion, then allow to cool.

Process the mushrooms with the lemon juice, ricotta, cream cheese and coriander until smooth. Season, to taste, then spoon into a serving dish. Cover and refrigerate for 2 hours to firm.

PREPARATION TIME: 15 MINUTES +   COOKING TIME: 5 MINUTES

NOTE: Large flat mushrooms have more flavour than the smaller button mushrooms. Choose firm, undamaged dry ones and store in a paper bag in the refrigerator.

MINI FRITTATAS

1 kg (2 lb 4 oz) orange sweet potato,
cut into small cubes
1 tablespoon oil
30 g (1 oz) butter
4 leeks, white part only, finely sliced
2 garlic cloves, crushed
250 g (9 oz) feta cheese, crumbled
8 eggs
125 ml (4 fl oz/½ cup) pouring (whipping)
cream

MAKES 12

Preheat the oven to 180°C (350°F/Gas 4). Grease two trays of six 250 ml (9 fl oz/1 cup) muffin holes. Cut small rounds of baking paper and place one into each hole.

Boil or steam the sweet potato until tender. Drain well and set aside.

Heat the oil and butter in a frying pan over low heat and cook the leek for 10 minutes, stirring occasionally, or until very soft and lightly golden. Add the garlic and cook for a further minute. Allow to cool, then stir in the feta and sweet potato. Divide the mixture among the muffin holes.

Whisk the eggs and cream together in a bowl and season with salt and cracked black pepper. Pour the egg mixture into each hole until three-quarters filled. Bake for 25-30 minutes, or until golden and set. Leave in the tins for 5 minutes, then ease out with a knife. Delicious served warm or at room temperature.

PREPARATION TIME: 30 MINUTES   COOKING TIME: 45 MINUTES

OYSTERS WITH BLOODY MARY SAUCE

24 oysters
60 ml (2 fl oz/¼ cup) tomato juice
2 teaspoons vodka
1 teaspoon lemon juice
½ teaspoon worcestershire sauce
1–2 drops of Tabasco sauce
1 celery stick
1–2 teaspoons snipped chives

SERVES 6

Remove the oysters from their shells. Clean and dry the shells. Combine the tomato juice, vodka, lemon juice, worcestershire sauce and Tabasco sauce in a small bowl.

Cut 1 celery stick into very thin julienne strips and place in the bases of the oyster shells. Top with an oyster and drizzle with tomato mixture. Sprinkle with 1–2 teaspoons snipped chives.

PREPARATION TIME: 20 MINUTES   COOKING TIME: NIL

PRAWN AND CHILLI PÂTÉ

750 g (1 lb 10 oz) raw prawns
(shrimp)
100 g (3½ oz) butter
2 garlic cloves, crushed
1 small green chilli, seeded and chopped
1 teaspoon finely grated lime zest
1 tablespoon lime juice
2 tablespoons whole-egg mayonnaise
2 tablespoons chopped coriander
(cilantro) leaves
Tabasco sauce, to taste (optional)

SERVES 6–8

Peel the prawns and gently pull out the dark vein from each prawn back, starting at the head end. Melt the butter in a large frying pan and add the garlic, chilli and prawns. Cook over medium heat for 10 minutes, or until tender.

Transfer the prawns to a food processor, add the lime zest and juice and process until the prawns are roughly chopped. Add the mayonnaise and coriander and stir through. Season with Tabasco sauce and salt and pepper, to taste. Spoon into a serving dish.

Chill for at least 1 hour, or until firm. Return to room temperature half an hour before serving. Serve with grissini, plain crackers or sweet chilli chips.

PREPARATION TIME: 30 MINUTES +   COOKING TIME: 10 MINUTES

NOTE: This pâté can be made a couple of days ahead.

Oysters with bloody mary sauce

BLACK SESAME SEED TARTS WITH MARINATED FETA

300 g (10½ oz) tomatoes
200 g (7 oz) feta cheese, diced
75 g (2½ oz/½ cup) black olives, pitted and diced
1 teaspoon finely chopped thyme
2 garlic cloves, crushed
1 tablespoon extra virgin olive oil
250 g (9 oz/2 cups) plain (all-purpose) flour
125 g (4½ oz) butter, chopped
60 g (2¼ oz) parmesan cheese, finely grated
1 tablespoon black sesame seeds
1 egg
extra thyme, to garnish

MAKES 30

Preheat the oven to 200°C (400°F/Gas 6). Lightly grease two 12-hole mini-muffin tins. Score a cross in the base of each tomato, place in a heatproof bowl and cover with boiling water. Leave for 30 seconds, then plunge in cold water. Peel away from the cross. Cut in half and scoop out the seeds with a teaspoon. Dice the flesh and combine in a bowl with the feta, olive, thyme, garlic and oil. Set aside.

Sift the flour into a large bowl and add the butter. Rub together with your fingertips until the mixture resembles fine breadcrumbs. Stir in the parmesan and sesame seeds. Make a well, add the egg and mix with a flat-bladed knife, using a cutting action until the mixture comes together in beads (add a little cold water if too dry).

On a lightly floured surface, press together into a ball, then wrap in plastic wrap and refrigerate for 10 minutes. Roll out to 2 mm (1/16 inch) thick between two sheets of baking paper. Remove the paper and cut out 30 rounds with a 6 cm (2½ inch) cutter. Gently press into the tins and bake for 10 minutes, or until dry and golden. Repeat with the remaining pastry rounds. Cool and place 1 heaped teaspoon feta filling into each pastry shell. Garnish and serve.

PREPARATION TIME: 25 MINUTES +   COOKING TIME: 20 MINUTES

TURKEY MEATBALLS WITH MINT YOGHURT

600 g (1 lb 5 oz) minced (ground) turkey
2 garlic cloves, crushed
2 tablespoons finely chopped mint
2 teaspoons finely chopped rosemary
2 tablespoons mango and lime chutney
2 tablespoons oil

MINT YOGHURT
200 g (7 oz) plain yoghurt
2 tablespoons finely chopped mint
2 teaspoons mango and lime chutney

MAKES 30

Mix the turkey, garlic, mint, rosemary and chutney in a bowl. With wet hands, roll tablespoons of the mixture into balls.

Heat half the oil in a large frying pan over medium heat and cook the balls, turning often, for 5 minutes or until cooked through. Drain on crumpled paper towels. Repeat with the remaining oil and meatballs.

Put the mint yoghurt ingredients together in a small bowl and stir until well combined. Serve with the turkey balls.

PREPARATION TIME: 15 MINUTES   COOKING TIME: 10 MINUTES

NOTE: You may need to order the minced (ground) turkey from a poultry specialist or you can use minced chicken instead.

PROSCIUTTO TWISTS

1 sheet of ready-made puff pastry, thawed
1 egg, beaten
8 slices prosciutto

MAKES 16

Preheat the oven to 210°C (415°F/Gas 6-7). Brush the sheet of puff pastry with a little of the beaten egg and cut into 1.5 cm (5/8 inch) wide strips. Holding both ends, twist the strips in opposite directions to create twists.

Place the twists on two lightly greased baking trays and bake for 10 minutes or until lightly browned and puffed. Remove from the trays and cool on a wire rack.

Cut the prosciutto into half lengthways, twist the prosciutto around the puff twists and serve.

PREPARATION TIME: 15 MINUTES   COOKING TIME: 10 MINUTES

DEVILS AND ANGELS ON HORSEBACK

4-6 bacon slices
12 pitted prunes
12 oysters, fresh or bottled
2 tablespoons worcestershire sauce
Tabasco sauce, to taste

MAKES 24

Soak 24 toothpicks in cold water for 30 minutes to prevent them burning. Cut each bacon slice into thin strips.

Wrap a piece of bacon around each prune and secure with a skewer.

Remove the oysters from their shells, or drain from the bottling liquid. Sprinkle lightly with worcestershire sauce and ground black pepper, to taste. Wrap each oyster in bacon, securing with a toothpick. Preheat a lightly greased grill or barbecue flatplate. Cook the savouries, turning occasionally, until the bacon is crisp. Serve sprinkled with a dash of Tabasco sauce.

PREPARATION TIME: 10 MINUTES +   COOKING TIME: 6 MINUTES

NOODLE NESTS WITH SMOKED SALMON TARTARE

200 g (7 oz) fresh flat egg noodles
olive oil, for brushing
200 g (7 oz) smoked salmon, diced
1 tablespoon extra virgin olive oil
3 teaspoons white wine vinegar
125 g (4½ oz/½ cup) whole-egg
mayonnaise
1 garlic clove, crushed
1 tablespoon finely chopped dill

MAKES 30

Preheat the oven to 200°C (400°F/Gas 6). Lightly grease three 12-hole mini-muffin tins. (You can use two 12-hole mini-muffin tins and cook the remaining six after the first batch is finished.) Use scissors or a sharp knife to cut the noodles into 10 cm (4 inch) lengths. Put the egg noodles in a heatproof bowl and pour boiling water over to cover. Soak for 5 minutes, then drain and pat dry with paper towels. Divide the noodles among 30 holes of the mini-muffin tins, pressing down to form 'nests'. Brush lightly with olive oil and bake for 15 minutes.

Turn out the noodles onto a wire rack, then put the rack in the oven for 5 minutes, or until the noodles are crisp.

Stir together the salmon, olive oil, vinegar, mayonnaise, garlic and dill in a bowl. Spoon 1 heaped teaspoon into each noodle nest and garnish with dill.

PREPARATION TIME: 25 MINUTES   COOKING TIME: 20 MINUTES

TARAMASALATA

4 slices white bread, crusts removed
60 ml (2 fl oz/¼ cup) milk
100 g (3½ oz) tarama or
smoked cod's roe
1 egg yolk
1 garlic clove, crushed
1 tablespoon grated onion
60 ml (2 fl oz/¼ cup) olive oil
80 ml (2½ fl oz/⅓ cup) lemon juice

SERVES 6

Soak the bread in the milk in a bowl for 5 minutes, then squeeze out the excess liquid.

Process the roe and egg yolk in a food processor for 10 seconds. Add the bread, garlic and onion and process for 20 seconds.

With the motor running, add the olive oil in a thin stream. Process until thick and creamy. Stir in the lemon juice before serving.

PREPARATION TIME: 25 MINUTES +   COOKING TIME: NIL

BRUSCHETTA WITH MEDITERRANEAN TOPPINGS

CAPSICUM (PEPPER) TOPPING
1 yellow capsicum (pepper)
1 red capsicum (pepper)
1 green capsicum (pepper)

TOMATO AND BASIL TOPPING
2 ripe tomatoes
3 tablespoons shredded basil
1 tablespoon extra virgin olive oil

12 slices crusty Italian bread
2 garlic cloves, halved
80 ml (2½ fl oz/⅓ cup) extra virgin olive oil
1 tablespoon chopped flat-leaf (Italian) parsley

MAKES 12

To make the capsicum topping, cut all the capsicums into large, flattish pieces and cook, skin side up, under a hot grill (broiler) until the skin blackens and blisters. Place in a plastic bag until cool, then peel. Slice the flesh into strips.

To make the tomato and basil topping, finely chop the tomatoes and combine in a bowl with the basil and olive oil. Season with black pepper.

Toast the bread and, while still hot, rub with the cut side of a garlic clove. Drizzle olive oil over each slice and sprinkle with salt and plenty of freshly ground black pepper.

Arrange the capsicum topping on half the bread slices, then sprinkle with parsley. Arrange the tomato and basil topping on the remaining bread slices. Serve immediately.

PREPARATION TIME: 20 MINUTES   COOKING TIME: 15 MINUTES

SEARED SALMON

600 g (1 lb 5 oz) salmon fillet
1 tablespoon cracked black pepper
1 teaspoon sea salt
2 tablespoons olive oil

SPICY COCKTAIL SAUCE
185 g (6½ oz/¾ cup) whole-egg
mayonnaise
3 tablespoons tomato sauce
2 teaspoons worcestershire sauce
1 teaspoon lemon juice
1 teaspoon sweet chilli sauce
2 teaspoons chopped flat-leaf
(Italian) parsley

SERVES 4–6

Remove the skin and bones from the salmon fillet and cut into 3 cm (1¼ inch) cubes and toss the cubes in the combined black pepper and sea salt. Heat the olive oil in a large frying pan and brown the salmon over high heat. Insert a toothpick in each piece and serve with the cocktail sauce.

To make the sauce, stir together the mayonnaise, tomato sauce, worcestershire sauce, lemon juice, sweet chilli sauce and parsley in a bowl.

PREPARATION TIME: 20 MINUTES   COOKING TIME: 15 MINUTES

THAI CHICKEN BALLS

1 kg (2 lb 4 oz) minced (ground) chicken
80 g (2¾ oz/1 cup) fresh breadcrumbs
4 spring onions (scallions), sliced
1 tablespoon ground coriander
50 g (1¾ oz/1 cup) chopped coriander
(cilantro) leaves
60 ml (2 fl oz/¼ cup) sweet chilli sauce
1–2 tablespoons lemon juice
oil, for shallow-frying

MAKES ABOUT 50 BALLS

Mix the chicken and breadcrumbs in a large bowl. Add the spring onion, ground and fresh coriander, chilli sauce and lemon juice, to taste, and mix well. With wet hands, form into evenly shaped walnut-sized balls. Preheat the oven to 200°C (400°F/Gas 6).

Heat 3 cm (1¼ inch) oil in a deep frying pan to 180°C (350°F), or until a cube of bread browns in 15 seconds, and shallow-fry the balls in batches over high heat until golden. Bake on a baking tray for 5 minutes, or until cooked through.

PREPARATION TIME: 20 MINUTES   COOKING TIME: 40 MINUTES

CUCUMBER ROUNDS WITH AVOCADO AND TURKEY

3 Lebanese (short) cucumbers
100 g (3½ oz) sliced smoked turkey
½ avocado, mashed
1 garlic clove, crushed
2 tablespoons cranberry sauce
2 tablespoons sour cream
cranberry sauce, extra, to garnish
alfalfa sprouts or mustard cress,
to garnish

MAKES 30

Slice the cucumbers into 1.5 cm (5/8 inch) rounds to make 30 pieces. Cut 30 rounds from the turkey using a 3 cm (1¼ inch) cutter.

Combine the avocado with the garlic, cranberry sauce and sour cream. Spoon 1 teaspoon onto each cucumber round and top with a round of turkey. Spoon a little cranberry sauce on top and garnish with alfalfa sprouts.

PREPARATION TIME: 20 MINUTES   COOKING TIME: NIL

Cucumber rounds with avocado and turkey

TEMPURA OCTOPUS

500 g (1 lb 2 oz) baby octopus
125 g (4½ oz/1 cup) tempura flour
oil, for deep-frying

GINGER AND ALMOND SAUCE
125 g (4½ oz/½ cup) sugar
60 ml (2 fl oz/¼ cup) white vinegar
60 ml (2 fl oz/¼ cup) lime juice
1 garlic clove, chopped
1 tablespoon freshly grated ginger
1 tablespoon chopped toasted
slivered almonds
1 tablespoon chopped coriander
(cilantro) leaves
1 tablespoon fish sauce

SERVES 4–6

Clean the octopus. First, remove the heads from the tentacles with a sharp knife. Push out the beaks from the centre of the tentacles, then cut the tentacles into sets of two or three.

Put the tempura flour into a bowl, make a well in the centre and stir in 185 ml (6 fl oz/¾ cup) iced water, until just combined.

Fill a large saucepan one-third full of oil and heat to 180°C (350°F), or until a cube of bread dropped in the oil browns in 15 seconds. Dip the octopus in the batter and deep-fry until golden. Drain on paper towels.

To make the sauce, put 125 ml (4 fl oz/½ cup) water, the sugar, vinegar, lime juice, garlic and ginger in a saucepan. Stir over low heat until the sugar has dissolved, then simmer for 5–8 minutes. Stir in the almonds, coriander and fish sauce. Serve hot or cold.

PREPARATION TIME: 20 MINUTES   COOKING TIME: 20 MINUTES

OYSTERS IN POTATOES WITH CHEESE SAUCE

24 baby new potatoes
15 g (½ oz) butter
½ small onion, finely chopped
1 tablespoon brandy
125 ml (4 fl oz/½ cup) pouring (whipping)
cream
30 g (1 oz/¼ cup) grated cheddar cheese
2 teaspoons chopped dill

SERVES 6–8

Cook the potatoes in boiling water for 5 minutes, or until tender. Drain and cool. Slice a round from the top of each potato and with a melon baller, scoop a ball from the centre of each. Trim the bases to sit flat.

Fill a saucepan one-third full of oil and heat to 180°C (350°F), or until a cube of bread dropped in the oil turns brown in 15 seconds. Deep-fry the potatoes until golden, then drain on paper towels.

Melt the butter in a saucepan, add the oysters and toss to seal. Remove from the pan. Add the onion to the pan and fry until soft. Add the brandy and, keeping away from anything flammable, ignite with a match. Allow the flames to die down. Add the cream, bring to the boil, then reduce the heat and simmer until thickened. Remove from the heat, stir in the cheddar and dill. Season. Return the oysters to the sauce, then spoon into the potatoes. Grill (broil) until golden brown. Sprinkle with dill.

PREPARATION TIME: 15 MINUTES   COOKING TIME: 25 MINUTES

TOMATO AND HALOUMI SKEWERS

500 g (1 lb 2 oz) haloumi cheese
5 large handfuls basil
150 g (5½ oz) semi-dried (sun-blushed) tomatoes
2 tablespoons balsamic vinegar
2 tablespoons extra virgin olive oil
1 teaspoon sea salt

MAKES 22

Preheat a barbecue hotplate or chargrill pan. Cut the cheese into 1.5 cm (5/8 inch) pieces. Thread a basil leaf onto a small skewer, followed by a piece of haloumi, a semi-dried tomato, another piece of haloumi and another basil leaf. Repeat to use the remaining ingredients.

Place the skewers on the barbecue hotplate and cook, turning occasionally until the cheese is golden brown, brushing with the combined vinegar and oil while cooking. Sprinkle with the salt and serve hot or warm.

PREPARATION TIME: 30 MINUTES   COOKING TIME: 10 MINUTES

NOTES: To make your own semi-dried (sun-blushed) tomatoes, preheat the oven to 160°C (315°F/Gas 2–3) and cut ripe roma (plum) tomatoes into quarters. Place on a wire rack and sit the rack on a baking tray. Sprinkle lightly with salt and pepper and a pinch of sugar. Bake for about 3–4 hours, until dry but still soft. The drying time will depend on the amount of moisture and the size of the tomatoes. Keep in an airtight container in the refrigerator for 4–5 days. Drizzle with olive oil, if desired.

PRAWN COCKTAILS

60 g (2¼ oz/¼ cup) whole-egg mayonnaise
2 teaspoons tomato sauce
dash of Tabasco sauce
¼ teaspoon worcestershire sauce
2 teaspoons thick (double/heavy) cream
¼ teaspoon lemon juice
24 cooked large prawns (shrimp)
4 lettuce leaves, shredded
lemon wedges, for serving

SERVES 4

Mix the mayonnaise, sauces, cream and juice together in a small bowl.

Peel the prawns, leaving the tails intact on eight of them. Gently pull out the dark vein from the back of each prawn, starting at the head end.

Divide the lettuce among four glasses. Arrange the prawns without the tails in the glasses and drizzle with the sauce. Hang two of the remaining prawns over the edge of each glass and serve with lemon wedges.

PREPARATION TIME: 20 MINUTES   COOKING TIME: NIL

MUSSELS WITH TOMATO SALSA

16–18 mussels
60 ml (2 fl oz/¼ cup) white wine
¼ small red onion, finely diced
1 small ripe tomato, finely diced
1 garlic clove, finely chopped
2 teaspoons balsamic vinegar
1 tablespoon virgin olive oil
1 tablespoon chopped basil

SERVES 4–6

Scrub 16–18 mussels with a stiff brush and pull out the hairy beards. Discard any broken mussels, or open ones that don't close when tapped on the bench. Rinse well.

Place 60 ml (2 fl oz/¼ cup) each of water and white wine in a saucepan and bring to the boil. Add the mussels, cover and cook over high heat for 3–5 minutes, until the mussels are open. Remove from the pan and discard any unopened mussels. Remove and discard one half of each mussel shell and loosen the mussels from the shells with a sharp knife.

Combine the onion, tomato, garlic, balsamic vinegar, olive oil and basil in a bowl. Season, to taste, and spoon over the mussels.

PREPARATION TIME: 15 MINUTES   COOKING TIME: 10 MINUTES

SEARED SCALLOPS WITH LIME

16 scallops
1 tablespoon vegetable oil
$^1/_4$-$^1/_2$ teaspoon sesame oil
1 tablespoon chopped chives
lime juice
chopped chives and toasted sesame
seeds, to serve

Remove 16 scallops from their shells and toss in a mixture of the oils and chives, then season with salt and pepper. Rinse and dry the shells.

Cook the scallops in a hot frying pan for 30 seconds on each side, or until just cooked through, being careful not to overcook. Return the scallops to the shells and squeeze some lime juice over the top. Sprinkle with chopped chives and toasted sesame seeds.

SERVES 4–6   PREPARATION TIME: 10 MINUTES   COOKING TIME: 5 MINUTES

MULLED WINE

12 cloves
2 oranges
60 g (2¼ oz/¼ cup) sugar
1 whole nutmeg, grated
4 cinnamon sticks
2 lemons, thinly sliced
750 ml (24 fl oz/3 cups) full-bodied red wine

SERVES 6

Push the cloves into the oranges and place in a saucepan with the sugar, nutmeg, cinnamon sticks and lemon. Pour in 500 ml (17 fl oz/2 cups) water and bring to the boil, then reduce the heat, cover the pan and simmer for 20 minutes. Allow to cool, then strain and discard the fruit and spices.

Pour the mixture into a saucepan, add the full-bodied red wine and heat until almost boiling — do not allow to boil or the alcohol will evaporate off. Serve in heatproof glasses.

EGGNOG

4 eggs, separated
90 g (3¼ oz/⅓ cup) caster (superfine) sugar
315 ml (10¾ fl oz/1¼ cups) hot milk
125 ml (4 fl oz/½ cup) bourbon
125 ml (4 fl oz/½ cup) pouring (whipping) cream
grated nutmeg, for sprinkling

SERVES 6–8

Beat the yolks and caster sugar in a heatproof bowl until light and fluffy. Add the hot milk and stir to combine.

Bring a saucepan of water to the boil and reduce the heat to simmer. Place the bowl over simmering water and stir with a wooden spoon for about 5–10 minutes, or until the mixture thickens and lightly coats the back of the spoon. Remove from the heat and allow to cool.

Stir in the bourbon. Beat the cream and the four egg whites separately until soft peaks form. Fold the cream, then the egg whites into the bourbon in two batches. Pour into glasses and sprinkle with grated nutmeg.

BUTTERED RUM

1 tablespoon sugar
250 ml (9 fl oz/1 cup) rum
1–2 teaspoons softened unsalted butter

SERVES 4

Place the sugar, rum and 500 ml (17 fl oz/2 cups) boiling water in a heatproof jug. Stir to dissolve the sugar, then divide among four mugs. Stir the butter into each mug and serve.

HOT TODDY

1 tablespoon soft brown sugar
4 slices of lemon
4 cinnamon sticks
12 whole cloves
125 ml (4 fl oz/½ cup) whisky

SERVES 4

Put the soft brown sugar, lemon, cinnamon sticks, cloves, whisky and 1 litre (35 fl oz/4 cups) boiling water in a heatproof jug. Stir to combine and leave to infuse for a few minutes, then strain. Add more sugar, to taste. Serve in heatproof glasses.

SANGRIA

2 tablespoons caster (superfine) sugar
1 tablespoon lemon juice
1 tablespoon orange juice
750 ml (26 fl oz/3 cups) chilled
red wine
ice cubes, to serve
1 orange, unpeeled, thinly sliced
1 lemon, unpeeled, thinly sliced
1 lime, unpeeled, thinly sliced

SERVES 6

Mix the caster sugar with the lemon and orange juice in a large bowl until the sugar has dissolved. Add the fruit slices to the bowl with the red wine and plenty of ice. Stir well until very cold. Serve in large wine glasses. (Do not strain.)

NOTES: This traditional Spanish drink can be made in large quantities, and its flavour will improve over several hours — it can be made up to a day in advance. Chopped seasonal fruits, such as peaches, pears and pineapples, can be added to this basic recipe. Good-quality wine is not essential in sangria, so use a table wine or even a cask wine.

BRANDY ALEXANDER PUNCH

750 ml (26 fl oz/3 cups) brandy
375 ml (13 fl oz/1½ cups) crème de cacao
(coffee liqueur)
1.75 litres (60 fl oz/7 cups) pouring
(whipping) cream
ice cubes, to serve
grated nutmeg, for sprinkling
strawberries, to garnish

SERVES 16

Pour the brandy, crème de cacao and cream into a large bowl. Whisk to just combine. Add ice cubes to a 3.5 litre (118 fl oz/14 cup) punch bowl and pour in the brandy mixture. Sprinkle with grated nutmeg, then serve in cocktail glasses garnished with strawberry halves.

BERRY AND CHERRY PUNCH

1 lemon
425 g (15 oz) tinned pitted black cherries
125 g (4½ oz) halved strawberries
600 g (1 lb 5 oz) assorted fresh or frozen berries
500 ml (17 fl oz/2 cups) lemonade
750 ml (26 fl oz/3 cups) ginger ale
250 ml (9 fl oz/1 cup) cold black tea
10 torn mint leaves
ice cubes, to serve

SERVES 10

Peel the skin from the lemon with a vegetable peeler, avoiding the bitter white pith. Cut into long thin strips.

Drain the black cherries and put in a large bowl. Add the strawberries, berries, lemonade, ginger ale, tea, mint leaves and the lemon zest. Cover and chill for at least 3 hours. Add ice cubes when serving.

SPARKLING PUNCH

250 ml (9 fl oz/1 cup) chilled pineapple juice
500 ml (17 fl oz/2 cups) chilled orange juice
500 ml (17 fl oz/2 cups) chilled apple cider
500 ml (17 fl oz/2 cups) chilled ginger ale
2 passionfruit
halved orange and lemon slices, to garnish
ice cubes, to serve

SERVES 6

Pour the pineapple juice and orange juice, apple cider and ginger ale into a large jug. Stir together, then stir in the flesh from the passionfruit. Garnish with halved orange and lemon slices. Ice cubes can be added to the jug or to each individual glass.

Berry and cherry punch

MAINS

ROAST TURKEY WITH COUNTRY SAGE STUFFING

3 kg (6 lb 12 oz) turkey
2 tablespoons oil
500 ml (17 fl oz/2 cups) chicken stock
2 tablespoons plain (all-purpose) flour

COUNTRY SAGE STUFFING
45 g (1½ oz) butter
1 onion, finely chopped
1 celery stick, sliced
10 large sage leaves, shredded
160 g (5½ oz/2 cups) fresh white breadcrumbs
1½ teaspoons dried sage
4 tablespoons finely chopped flat-leaf (Italian) parsley
2 egg whites, lightly beaten
1 teaspoon salt
½ teaspoon white pepper

SERVES 6–8

Remove the neck and giblets from inside the turkey. Wash the turkey well and pat dry inside and out with paper towels. Preheat the oven to 180°C (350°F/Gas 4).

To make the stuffing, melt the butter in a small saucepan and cook the onion and celery over medium heat for 3 minutes, or until the onion has softened. Transfer to a bowl and add the sage leaves, breadcrumbs, dried sage, parsley, egg whites, salt and white pepper. Loosely stuff into the turkey cavity. Tuck the wings underneath and join the cavity with a skewer. Tie the legs together. Place on a rack in a baking dish. Roast for 2 hours, basting with the combined oil and 125 ml (4 fl oz/ ½ cup) of the stock. Cover the breast and legs with foil after 1 hour if the turkey is overbrowning. Remove from the oven, cover and leave to rest for 15 minutes.

To make the gravy, drain off all except 2 tablespoons of pan juices from the baking dish. Place the dish on the stove over low heat, add the flour and stir well. Stir over medium heat until browned. Gradually add the remaining stock, stirring until the gravy boils and thickens. Serve the turkey with gravy and roast vegetables.

PREPARATION TIME: 45 MINUTES   COOKING TIME: 2 HOURS

NOTE: Do not stuff the turkey until you are ready to cook it. Stuffing can be made ahead of time and frozen for up to a month in an airtight container. If you prefer to cook the stuffing separately, press it lightly into a lightly greased ovenproof dish and bake for about 30 minutes, or until golden brown. Small greased muffin tins can also be used (bake for 15–20 minutes). Alternatively, you can form the mixture into balls and fry in a little melted butter or oil, over medium heat, until golden brown all over.

PEPPERED BEEF FILLET WITH BÉARNAISE SAUCE

1 kg (2 lb 4 oz) beef eye fillet
1 tablespoon oil
2 garlic cloves, crushed
1 tablespoon cracked black peppercorns
2 teaspoons crushed coriander seeds

BÉARNAISE SAUCE
3 spring onions (scallions), chopped
125 ml (4 fl oz/½ cup) dry white wine
2 tablespoons tarragon vinegar
1 tablespoon chopped tarragon
125 g (4½ oz) butter
4 egg yolks
1 tablespoon lemon juice

SERVES 6

Preheat the oven to 210°C (415°F/Gas 6–7). Trim the fillet, removing any excess fat. Tie at regular intervals with kitchen string. Combine the oil and garlic, brush over the fillet, then roll the fillet in the combined peppercorns and coriander seeds.

Put the meat on a rack in a baking dish. Bake for 10 minutes, then reduce the oven to 180°C (350°F/Gas 4) and cook for a further 15–20 minutes for a rare result, or until cooked according to taste. Cover and leave for 10–15 minutes.

To make the béarnaise sauce, put the spring onion, wine, vinegar and tarragon in a saucepan. Boil the mixture until only 2 tablespoons of the liquid remains. Strain and set aside. Melt the butter in a small saucepan. Place the wine mixture in a food processor with the egg yolks, and process for 30 seconds. With the motor running, add the butter in a thin stream, leaving the milky white sediment behind in the saucepan. Process until thickened. Add the lemon juice, to taste, and season.

PREPARATION TIME: 30 MINUTES   COOKING TIME: 45 MINUTES

HERBED POUSSINS

135 g (4¾ oz) butter, softened
2 teaspoons chopped lemon thyme
1 tablespoon chopped flat-leaf (Italian) parsley
2 spring onions (scallions), finely chopped
1 teaspoon finely grated lemon zest
1½ tablespoons lemon juice
4 x 500 g (1 lb 2 oz) poussins (baby chickens)
30 g (1 oz) butter, melted, extra
2 teaspoons lemon juice, extra

SERVES 4

Mix the softened butter with the herbs, spring onion, lemon zest, lemon juice, and plenty of salt and pepper.

Preheat the oven to 200°C (400°F/Gas 6). Cut the chickens down either side of the backbone. Discard the backbone, and gently flatten the chickens. Carefully lift the skin from the breastbone and the legs and push the butter underneath. Tuck in the wings and neck.

Place the chickens on a rack in a baking dish. Brush with the combined extra butter and extra lemon juice. Bake for 30–35 minutes, or until the juices run clear.

PREPARATION TIME: 30 MINUTES   COOKING TIME: 35 MINUTES

Peppered beef fillet with béarnaise sauce

HONEY-GLAZED HAM

7 kg (15 lb) smoked, cooked leg ham

HONEY GLAZE
125 g (4½ oz/⅔ cup) soft brown sugar
3 tablespoons honey
1 tablespoon hot English mustard

SERVES 20

Preheat the oven to 180°C (350°F/Gas 4). Cut a line through the thick rind of the leg ham, 6 cm (2½ inches) from the shank end so you can easily lift the rind. To remove the rind, run your thumb around the edge, under the rind and carefully pull back, easing your hand under the rind between the fat and the rind. With a sharp knife, lightly score the fat to form a diamond pattern. Do not cut all the way through to the ham or the fat will fall off during cooking.

To make the honey glaze, mix the sugar, honey and mustard together in a bowl. Spread half the glaze over the ham with a palette knife or the back of a spoon and press a clove into the centre of each diamond.

Put the ham on a rack in a deep baking dish and pour 500 ml (17 fl oz/ 2 cups) water into the dish. Cover the ham and dish securely with greased foil and cook for 45 minutes. Remove from the oven and brush or spread the remaining glaze over the ham. Increase the heat to 210°C (415°F/Gas 6–7) and bake, uncovered, for 20 minutes, or until the surface is lightly caramelized. Set aside for 15 minutes before carving.

PREPARATION TIME: 20 MINUTES   COOKING TIME: 1 HOUR 5 MINUTES

MINTED RACKS OF LAMB

4 x 4-cutlet racks of lamb
300 g (10½ oz/1 cup) mint jelly
2 tablespoons white wine
3 tablespoons finely chopped chives

SERVES 4

Preheat the oven to 200°C (400°F/Gas 6). Trim any excess fat from the lamb, leaving a thin layer of fat, and clean any meat or sinew from the ends of the bones using a small sharp knife. Cover the bones with foil. Place on a rack in a baking dish.

Mix the mint jelly and white wine together in a saucepan over high heat. Bring to the boil and boil for 4 minutes, or until the mixture is reduced and thickened. Cool slightly, add the chives, then brush over the racks of lamb. Bake the lamb for 15–20 minutes for rare, or 35 minutes if you prefer medium-rare, brushing with glaze every 10 minutes. Remove the foil and leave the lamb to stand for 5 minutes before serving with vegetables.

PREPARATION TIME: 15 MINUTES   COOKING TIME: 45 MINUTES

ROAST TURKEY BREAST WITH PARSLEY CRUST

60 g (2¼ oz) butter
4 spring onions (scallions), finely chopped
2 garlic cloves, crushed
160 g (5¾ oz/2 cups) white breadcrumbs
2 tablespoons chopped flat-leaf (Italian) parsley
1 kg (2 lb 4 oz) turkey breast
1 egg, lightly beaten

RASPBERRY AND REDCURRANT SAUCE
150 g (5½ oz) fresh or frozen raspberries
60 ml (2 fl oz/¼ cup) orange juice
160 g (5¾ oz/½ cup) cranberry sauce
2 teaspoons dijon mustard
1 teaspoon finely grated orange zest
60 ml (2 fl oz/¼ cup) port

SERVES 8

Melt the butter in a frying pan over medium heat. Add the onion and garlic and stir until softened. Add the breadcrumbs and parsley and stir until combined. Allow to cool.

Preheat the oven to 180°C (350°F/Gas 4). Place the turkey in a deep baking dish. Brush with egg. Press the parsley crust onto the turkey. Bake for 45 minutes, or until the crust is golden. Serve sliced, with raspberry and redcurrant sauce.

To make the sauce, press the raspberries through a sieve to remove the seeds. Combine the purée in a saucepan with orange juice, cranberry sauce, mustard and orange zest. Stir until smooth. Add port and simmer for 5 minutes. Remove and allow to cool.

PREPARATION TIME: 10 MINUTES   COOKING TIME: 45 MINUTES

ROAST CHICKEN WITH BACON AND SAGE STUFFING

2 x 1.2 kg (2 lb 12 oz) chickens
4 bacon slices
2 tablespoons oil
1 small onion, finely chopped
1 tablespoon chopped sage
125 g (4½ oz/1½ cups) fresh breadcrumbs
1 egg, lightly beaten

WINE GRAVY
2 tablespoons plain (all-purpose) flour
2 teaspoons worcestershire sauce
2 tablespoons red or white wine
560 ml (19¼ fl oz/2¼ cups) beef or chicken stock

SERVES 6

Preheat the oven to 180°C (350°F/Gas 4). Remove the giblets and any large fat deposits from the chickens. Wipe over and pat dry inside and out with paper towels.

Finely chop two of the bacon slices. Heat half the oil in a small frying pan. Add the onion and the finely chopped bacon and cook until the onion is soft and the bacon is starting to brown. Transfer to a bowl and cool. Add the sage, breadcrumbs and egg to the onion, season, to taste, and mix lightly. Spoon some stuffing into each chicken cavity.

Fold the wings back and tuck under the chickens. Tie the legs of each chicken together with string. Place the chickens on a rack in a large baking dish, making sure they are not touching, and brush with some of the remaining oil. Pour 250 ml (9 fl oz/1 cup) water into the baking dish.

Cut the remaining bacon into long, thin strips and lay across the chicken breasts. Brush the bacon with oil. Bake for 45-60 minutes, or until the juices run clear when a thigh is pierced with a skewer.

To make the gravy, discard all but 2 tablespoons of the pan juices from the baking dish you cooked the roast in. Heat the dish on the stovetop over medium heat, stir in the flour and cook, stirring, until well browned. Remove from the heat and gradually add the worcestershire sauce, wine and stock. Return to the heat, stir until the mixture boils and thickens, then simmer for 2 minutes. Season with salt and pepper, to taste.

PREPARATION TIME: 15 MINUTES   COOKING TIME: 1 HOUR 10 MINUTES

Roast chicken with bacon and sage stuffing

SEAFOOD PIE

2 tablespoons olive oil
3 large onions, thinly sliced
1 fennel bulb, thinly sliced
600 ml (21 fl oz) fish stock
750 ml (26 fl oz/3 cups) pouring (whipping) cream
1 tablespoon brandy
750 g (1 lb 10 oz) skinless snapper fillets, cut into large pieces
250 g (9 oz) scallops
500 g (1 lb 2 oz) raw prawns (shrimp), peeled and deveined
2 tablespoons chopped flat-leaf (Italian) parsley
2 sheets ready-rolled puff pastry
1 egg, lightly beaten

SERVES 8

Preheat the oven to 220°C (425°F/Gas 7). Heat the oil in a deep frying pan, add the onion and fennel and cook over medium heat for 20 minutes or until caramelized.

Add the stock to the pan and bring to the boil. Cook until the liquid is almost evaporated. Stir in the cream and brandy, bring to the boil, then reduce the heat and simmer for 10 minutes, or until reduced by half. Add the seafood and parsley and toss for 3 minutes.

Lightly grease a 2.5 litre (84 fl oz/10 cup) pie dish and add the seafood mixture. Arrange the pastry over the top to cover, trim the excess and press down around the edges. Decorate with any trimmings. Make a steam hole in the top and brush the pastry with egg. Bake for 30 minutes, or until cooked through and the pastry is crisp and golden.

PREPARATION TIME: 20 MINUTES   COOKING TIME: 1 HOUR 20 MINUTES

HAM AND CIDER CASSEROLE

40 g (1½ oz) butter
1 onion, chopped
2 leeks, white part only, finely sliced
2 garlic cloves, crushed
8 slices ham, chopped
100 ml (3½ fl oz) apple cider
300 g (10½ oz) tinned butter beans, rinsed and drained
25 g (1 oz/⅓ cup) fresh breadcrumbs
1 tablespoon grated parmesan cheese

SERVES 4

Preheat the oven to 200°C (400°F/Gas 6). Melt half the butter in a heavy-based frying pan, add the onion and cook over low heat for 2–3 minutes, or until tender. Add the leek and stir until cooked through. Stir in the garlic.

Transfer the onion mixture to an ovenproof dish. Scatter the ham over the top and season with freshly ground black pepper. Pour in the apple cider. Spoon the butter beans over and around the ham and sprinkle with the breadcrumbs and parmesan. Dot with the remaining butter and bake for 20 minutes, or until lightly golden on top.

PREPARATION TIME: 15 MINUTES   COOKING TIME: 25 MINUTES

BEEF WELLINGTON

1.2 kg (2 lb 12 oz) beef fillet or rib-eye in
1 piece
1 tablespoon oil
125 g (4$\frac{1}{2}$ oz) pâté
60 g (2$\frac{1}{4}$ oz) button mushrooms, sliced
375 g (13 oz) block puff pastry, thawed
1 egg, lightly beaten
1 sheet ready-rolled puff pastry, thawed

SERVES 6–8

Preheat the oven to 210°C (415°F/Gas 6-7). Trim the meat of any excess fat and sinew. Fold the thinner part of the tail end under the meat and tie securely with kitchen string at regular intervals to form an even shape.

Rub the meat with freshly ground black pepper. Heat the oil over high heat in a large frying pan. Add the meat and brown well all over. Remove from the heat and allow to cool. Remove the string.

Spread the pâté over the top and sides of the beef. Cover with the mushrooms, pressing them onto the pâté. Roll out the block pastry on a lightly floured surface to a rectangle large enough to completely enclose the beef.

Place the beef on the pastry, brush the edges with egg, and fold over to enclose the meat completely, brushing the edges of the pastry with the beaten egg to seal, and folding in the ends. Invert onto a greased baking tray so the seam is underneath. Cut leaf shapes from the sheet of puff pastry and use to decorate the Wellington. Use the egg to stick on the shapes. Cut a few slits in the top to allow the steam to escape. Brush the top and sides of the pastry with egg, and cook for 45 minutes for rare, 1 hour for medium or 1$\frac{1}{2}$ hours for well done. Leave in a warm place for 10 minutes before cutting into slices for serving.

PREPARATION TIME: 25 MINUTES   COOKING TIME: 1 HOUR 30 MINUTES

NOTE: Use a firm pâté, discarding any jelly. Cover the pastry loosely with foil if it begins to darken too much.

Beef wellington

ROAST PHEASANT

2 x 1 kg (2 lb 4 oz) pheasants
6 thin bacon slices
8 sprigs thyme
2 large pieces of muslin
80 g (2¾ oz) butter, melted
2 apples, cored and cut into
thick wedges
60 ml (2 fl oz/¼ cup) apple cider
125 ml (4 fl oz/½ cup) pouring (whipping)
cream
2 teaspoons thyme leaves
2-4 teaspoons apple cider vinegar

SERVES 4-6

Preheat the oven to 230°C (450°C/Gas 8). Rinse the pheasants and pat dry. Tuck the wings underneath the pheasants and tie the legs together with kitchen string. Wrap the bacon around each pheasant and secure with toothpicks. Thread the thyme sprigs through the bacon. Dip the pieces of muslin into the melted butter and wrap one around each pheasant.

Place on a rack in a baking dish and bake for 10 minutes. Reduce the oven to 200°C (400°C/Gas 6) and bake for a further 35 minutes. About 20 minutes before the end of the cooking, add the apple wedges to the base of the dish. The pheasants are cooked when the juices run clear when pierced with a skewer. Remove the pheasants and apple wedges, discard the muslin and toothpicks, then cover and keep warm.

Place the baking dish with the juices on the stovetop. Pour the apple cider into the pan and bring to the boil. Cook for 3 minutes, or until reduced by half. Strain into a clean saucepan. Add the cream to the saucepan and boil for 5 minutes, or until the sauce thickens slightly. Stir in the thyme leaves and season well. Add the apple cider vinegar, to taste. Serve with the pheasant and apple.

PREPARATION TIME: 20 MINUTES   COOKING TIME: 1 HOUR

VEAL FOYOT

50 g (1¾ oz) butter
1 onion, chopped
185 ml (6 fl oz/¾ cup) white wine
185 ml (6 fl oz/¾ cup) beef stock
1.5 kg (3 lb 5 oz) nut (cushion) of veal
80 g (2¾ oz/1 cup) fresh breadcrumbs
125 g (4½ oz) gruyère cheese, grated

SERVES 6

Preheat the oven to 180°C (350°F/Gas 4). Melt half the butter in a saucepan and fry the onion until soft. Add the wine and stock, bring to the boil and boil for 2 minutes. Add ¼ teaspoon each of salt and white pepper. Remove from the heat and allow to cool.

Place the veal in a baking dish and rub with salt and white pepper. Pour the onion and wine mixture into the baking dish with the veal. Mix the breadcrumbs and cheese, and press firmly on the veal to form a thick coating. Melt the remaining butter and pour over the cheese crust.

Roast the veal for 1¼-1½ hours. If the crust is browning too quickly, cover lightly with foil. Leave for 10 minutes before carving into 1 cm (½ inch) slices. Spoon pan juices over the top.

PREPARATION TIME: 25 MINUTES   COOKING TIME: 1 HOUR 35 MINUTES

BAKED SALMON

2 kg (4 lb 8 oz) Atlantic salmon, cleaned, gutted and scaled
2 spring onions (scallions), roughly chopped
3 dill sprigs
½ lemon, thinly sliced
6 black peppercorns
60 ml (2 fl oz/¼ cup) dry white wine
3 bay leaves
lemon wedges, to serve

SERVES 8

Preheat the oven to 180°C (350°F/Gas 4). If the salmon is too long for your baking dish, remove the head. Rinse the salmon under cold running water and pat dry inside and out with paper towels. Stuff the cavity with the spring onion, dill, lemon slices and peppercorns.

Brush a large double-layered piece of foil with oil and lay the salmon on the foil. Sprinkle the wine all over the salmon and arrange the bay leaves over the top. Fold the foil over and wrap up tightly.

Bake in a shallow baking dish for 30 minutes. Turn the oven off and leave the salmon in the oven for 45 minutes with the door closed. Do not open or remove the foil during the cooking or standing time.

Undo the foil and carefully peel away the skin of the salmon on the top side. Carefully flip the salmon onto the serving plate and remove the skin from the other side. Pull out the fins and any visible bones. Serve at room temperature with lemon wedges.

PREPARATION TIME: 10 MINUTES   COOKING TIME: 30 MINUTES

NOTE: This is delicious served with tarragon mayonnaise. Put 2 egg yolks, 1 teaspoon dijon mustard and 2 teaspoons lemon juice in a food processor and process for 10 seconds. With the motor running, add 250 ml (9 fl oz/1 cup) light olive oil in a slow, thin stream until combined. Stir in 2 teaspoons of lemon juice, 2 teaspoons of chopped tarragon and season with salt and white pepper.

STANDING RIB ROAST WITH PÂTÉ

1 bacon slice, chopped
1 onion, finely chopped
125 g (4½ oz) mushrooms, finely chopped
50 g (1¾ oz/½ cup) dry breadcrumbs
125 g (4½ oz) pâté
2 tablespoons chopped flat-leaf
(Italian) parsley
1 teaspoon chopped oregano
1 egg, lightly beaten
4 kg (9 lb) standing rib roast (6 chops)

SERVES 6

Preheat the oven to 240°C (475°F/Gas 9). Place the bacon in a dry frying pan, and cook until it begins to soften and release its fat. Add the onion and mushroom and cook, stirring, for 3 minutes. Transfer to a bowl and mix in the breadcrumbs, pâté, parsley, oregano and egg. Season.

Cut a slit in the meat, between the rib bones and the meat. Spoon the pâté mixture into the slit. Secure the meat with string. Place the meat in a baking dish, fat side up. Bake for 15 minutes, then reduce the heat to 180°C (350°F/Gas 4). Bake for a further 1½ hours for rare, or up to 2 hours for medium, or until cooked according to taste. Allow the meat to rest for 15 minutes before carving. Remove the string and cut the meat into thick slices, allowing one bone per person.

PREPARATION TIME: 30 MINUTES   COOKING TIME: 2 HOURS 20 MINUTES

QUAILS WITH BACON AND ROSEMARY

8 quails
1 onion, chopped
3 bacon slices, chopped
1 tablespoon fresh rosemary leaves
30 g (1 oz) butter, melted
125 ml (4 fl oz/½ cup) port
125 ml (4 fl oz/½ cup) pouring (whipping)
cream
1 teaspoon cornflour (cornstarch)

SERVES 4

Preheat the oven to 200°C (400°F/Gas 6). Wash the quails, then dry inside and out with paper towels. Tuck the wings underneath the quails and tie the legs close to the body with kitchen string.

Spread the onion, bacon and rosemary over the base of a baking dish, and add the quails. Brush each quail with the melted butter. Combine the port with 60 ml (2 fl oz/¼ cup) of water, then pour 125 ml (4 fl oz/½ cup) of this mixture over the quails. Bake for about 25 minutes, or until the juices run clear when the quails are pierced in the thigh with a skewer. Cover and leave for 10 minutes.

Carefully strain any juices from the baking dish into a small saucepan, reserving the rosemary and bacon mixture. Add the remaining port and water mixture to the pan, and bring to the boil. Reduce the heat and gradually stir in the blended cream and cornflour, stirring until slightly thickened. Serve the quails with the sauce and the reserved rosemary and bacon mixture.

PREPARATION TIME: 30 MINUTES   COOKING TIME: 35 MINUTES

Standing rib roast with pâté

TURKEY ROLL WITH MANDARIN SAUCE

3.4 kg (7 lb 13 oz) turkey
90 g (3¼ oz) dried apricots, chopped
30 g (1 oz) butter
1 onion, finely chopped
1 garlic clove, crushed
400 g (14 oz) minced (ground) chicken
120 g (4 oz/1½ cups) fresh breadcrumbs
35 g (1¼ oz/½ cup) currants
35 g (1¼ oz/½ cup) pistachio nuts, toasted and chopped
3 tablespoons chopped flat-leaf (Italian) parsley

MANDARIN SAUCE
2 mandarins
1 tablespoon long thin strips of mandarin zest
2 tablespoons sugar
1 tablespoon brandy
250 ml (9 fl oz/1 cup) mandarin juice
80 ml (2½ fl oz/⅓ cup) chicken stock
3 teaspoons cornflour (cornstarch)
1 spring onion (scallion), finely sliced

SERVES 8

To bone the turkey, cut through the skin on the centre back with a sharp knife or pair of scissors. Separate the flesh from the bone down one side to the breast, being careful not to pierce the skin. Follow along the rib cage closely with the knife, gradually easing the meat from the bones. Repeat on the other side, then lift the rib cage away, leaving the flesh in one piece and the drumsticks still attached to the flesh. Cut off the wing tips and scrape all the meat from the drumsticks and wings, discarding the bones. Turn the wing and drumstick flesh inside the turkey and lay the turkey out flat, skin side down. Refrigerate.

Place the apricot in a small bowl, cover with boiling water and soak for 30 minutes. Preheat the oven to 180°C (350°F/Gas 4).

Meanwhile, melt the butter in a frying pan, add the onion and garlic and cook, stirring, for about 5 minutes, or until the onion is soft. Remove from the heat. Combine the mince, onion mixture, breadcrumbs, currants, nuts, parsley and apricot in a bowl and mix well. Season. Place the turkey on the work surface, skin side down and form the stuffing mixture into a large sausage shape about the same length as the turkey. Fold the turkey over to enclose the stuffing. Secure with toothpicks or skewers and truss with kitchen string at 3 cm (1¼ inch) intervals.

Place on a lightly greased baking tray. Rub with a little extra oil and season. Roast the turkey roll for 1½–2 hours, or until the juices run clear. Cover and set aside for 10 minutes while preparing the sauce. Carefully remove the string and toothpicks. Cut into slices and serve with the mandarin sauce.

To make the mandarin sauce, segment the mandarins. Remove the zest and white pith, then cut between the membranes to release the segments. Place the zest in a saucepan, cover with water and bring to the boil. Drain and repeat. Sprinkle the sugar over the base of a saucepan over medium heat and stir until all the sugar has dissolved. Remove from the heat, cool, then stir in the brandy. Return to the heat, stir to dissolve any toffee, then add the combined mandarin juice and chicken stock. Add the combined cornflour and 1 tablespoon water and stir over heat until the mixture thickens. Add the mandarin segments and zest, stirring until heated through. Stir in the spring onion, then season.

PREPARATION TIME: 1 HOUR +   COOKING TIME: 2 HOURS

LOBSTER WITH PARSLEY MAYONNAISE

2 cooked rock lobsters
mixed lettuce leaves, lemon wedges
and snipped chives, to serve

PARSLEY MAYONNAISE
40 g (1½ oz) parsley sprigs, stalks
removed, finely chopped
3 teaspoons dijon mustard
1 teaspoon honey
1 tablespoon lemon juice
60 ml (2 fl oz/¼ cup) pouring (whipping)
cream
60 g (2¼ oz/¼ cup) mayonnaise

SERVES 4

Cut each lobster in half lengthways through the shell. Lift the meat from the tail and body. Crack the legs and prise the meat from them. Remove the cream-coloured vein and soft body matter and discard. Cut the lobster meat into 2 cm (¾ inch) pieces, cover and refrigerate.

To make the parsley mayonnaise, put the parsley, mustard, honey, lemon juice, cream and mayonnaise in a food processor. Blend until combined, then season. Spoon the mixture into a bowl, cover and refrigerate.

Place a bed of lettuce on each serving plate, top with slices of lobster and spoon parsley mayonnaise over the top.

PREPARATION TIME: 25 MINUTES   COOKING TIME: NIL

ROAST CHICKEN WITH RICE STUFFING

95 g (3¼ oz/½ cup) wild rice
15 pitted prunes, quartered
2 tablespoons port
60 g (2¼ oz) butter
4 spring onions (scallions),
finely chopped
45 g (1½ oz/⅓ cup) hazelnuts, roasted
and roughly chopped
½ green apple, coarsely grated
½ teaspoon grated orange zest
½ teaspoon ground cardamom
1 egg, lightly beaten
1.5 kg (3 lb 5 oz) chicken

SERVES 4

Put the rice in a saucepan and add enough boiling water to come 2.5 cm (1 inch) above the rice. Bring to the boil, reduce the heat and simmer for 10 minutes. Remove from the heat, cover and leave for 1 hour, then drain.

Preheat the oven to 180°C (350°F/Gas 4). Combine the prunes and port in a bowl, cover and set aside. Melt half the butter in a saucepan and add the spring onion. Cook over low heat, stirring, for 2 minutes or until soft. Remove from the heat and mix in the rice, prune and port mixture, hazelnuts, apple, orange zest, cardamom and beaten egg. Season.

Wipe the chicken and pat dry. Spoon the stuffing into the cavity and secure with a toothpick. Tuck the wings under the chicken and tie the drumsticks together with string. Place on a rack in a baking dish. Melt the remaining butter and brush over the chicken. Bake for 1 hour 15 minutes, or until brown. Cover with foil and leave for 10 minutes. Remove the toothpicks and string before carving.

PREPARATION TIME: 20 MINUTES   COOKING TIME: 1 HOUR 35 MINUTES

GAME PIE

1 kg (2 lb 4 oz) rabbit, boned, cut into
bite-sized pieces
1.25 kg (2 lb 12 oz) diced venison
30 g (1 oz/1/4 cup) plain (all-purpose) flour
2–3 tablespoons oil
2 bacon slices, chopped
1 onion, sliced into thin wedges
2 garlic cloves, crushed
150 g (51/2 oz) button mushrooms,
cut in halves
250 ml (9 fl oz/1 cup) red wine
250 ml (9 fl oz/1 cup) beef stock
3 sprigs thyme
2 bay leaves
185 g (61/2 oz) puff pastry, thawed
1 egg yolk
2 tablespoons milk

SERVES 4–6

Lightly coat the rabbit and venison in seasoned flour. Heat the oil in a large saucepan and cook the bacon over medium heat until golden. Remove. Brown the meats well in batches, remove and set aside. Add the onion and garlic to the saucepan and cook until browned.

Return the bacon and meat to the saucepan and add the mushrooms, wine, stock, thyme and bay leaves. Bring to the boil, then reduce the heat and simmer over low heat, stirring occasionally, for 1½ hours, or until the meat is tender. Transfer to a heatproof bowl. Remove the thyme and bay leaves. Refrigerate until cold.

Preheat the oven to 200°C (400°F/Gas 6). Spoon the mixture into a 2 litre (70 fl oz/8 cup) ovenproof dish. Roll out the half block of pastry on a lightly floured surface to about 5 mm (1/4 inch) thick. Cut strips the width of the pie dish rim and secure to the dish with a little water. Reserve the leftover pastry. Roll the other block of pastry on a lightly floured surface until large enough to fit the top of the pie dish. Brush the edges of the pastry strips with a little combined egg yolk and milk. Drape the pastry over the rolling pin and lower it onto the top of the pie. Trim off any excess pastry using a sharp knife. Score the edges of the pastry with the back of a knife to seal. Use any leftover pastry to decorate the top. Cut two slits in the top of the pastry and brush all over with the remaining egg and milk mixture. Bake for 30–40 minutes, or until puffed and golden.

PREPARATION TIME: 40 MINUTES +   COOKING TIME: 2 HOURS 30 MINUTES

NOTES: Ask the butcher to bone the rabbit. Order the venison from the butcher.

HERBED RACK OF VEAL

1.2 kg (2 lb 12 oz) rack of veal (8 cutlets)
80 g (2³/4 oz/1 cup) fresh breadcrumbs
50 g (1³/4 oz/¹/2 cup) dry breadcrumbs
1 tablespoon chopped flat-leaf
(Italian) parsley
1 tablespoon chopped basil
2 egg whites, lightly beaten
2 garlic cloves, crushed
1 tablespoon oil
30 g (1 oz) butter, melted

LEMON SAUCE
80 ml (2¹/2 fl oz/¹/3 cup) dry white wine
2 tablespoons lemon juice
2 teaspoons sugar
125 ml (4 fl oz/¹/2 cup) pouring (whipping)
cream
60 g (2¹/4 oz) chilled butter, cubed
1 tablespoon chopped flat-leaf
(Italian) parsley

SERVES 4–6

Preheat the oven to 160°C (315°F/Gas 2–3). Trim the veal of excess fat. Combine all the breadcrumbs, parsley and basil in a bowl. Add the combined egg whites, garlic, oil and butter, and mix. Press the mixture firmly over the meat and place in a baking dish, crust side up. Bake for 1¹/4 hours for medium, or 1¹/2 hours for well done.

Remove the meat from the pan and leave for 10 minutes. Drain off all except 2 tablespoons of pan juices.

To make the lemon sauce, put the baking dish with the reserved pan juices on the stovetop. Add 125 ml (4 fl oz/¹/2 cup) water with the wine, lemon juice, sugar and cream. Bring to the boil, then reduce the heat. Simmer for 5–7 minutes, or until the mixture is reduced by about 125 ml (4 fl oz/¹/2 cup). Remove from the heat and whisk in the butter, one cube at a time, then strain and stir in the parsley. Cut the veal rack into cutlets and serve with the lemon sauce.

PREPARATION TIME: 45 MINUTES   COOKING TIME: 1 HOUR 40 MINUTES

ROAST LEG OF LAMB WITH GARLIC AND ROSEMARY

2 kg (4 lb 8 oz) leg of lamb
2 garlic cloves, cut into thin slivers
2 tablespoons rosemary sprigs
2 teaspoons oil

MINT SAUCE
3 tablespoons caster (superfine) sugar
10 g (¹/4 oz/¹/2 cup) mint leaves
185 ml (6 fl oz/³/4 cup) malt vinegar

SERVES 6

Preheat the oven to 180°C (350°F/Gas 4). Cut small slits all over the lamb. Insert the garlic and rosemary into the slits. Brush the lamb with the oil and season. Place on a rack in a baking dish. Add 125 ml (4 fl oz/ ¹/2 cup) water to the dish. Bake for about 1 hour 30 minutes for medium, or until cooked as desired, basting often with the pan juices. Keep warm and leave for 10–15 minutes before carving. Serve with mint sauce.

To make the mint sauce, sprinkle 1 tablespoon of the sugar over the mint leaves on a chopping board, then finely chop the mint. Transfer to a bowl and add the remaining sugar. Cover with 60 ml (2 fl oz/¹/4 cup) boiling water and stir until the sugar has dissolved. Stir in the malt vinegar, cover and chill overnight.

PREPARATION TIME: 20 MINUTES   COOKING TIME: 1 HOUR 30 MINUTES

ROAST PORK FILLET WITH APPLE AND MUSTARD SAUCE AND GLAZED APPLES

750 g (1 lb 10 oz) pork fillet
30 g (1 oz) butter
1 tablespoon oil
1 garlic clove, crushed
$\frac{1}{2}$ teaspoon freshly grated ginger
1 tablespoon seeded mustard
60 ml (2 fl oz/$\frac{1}{4}$ cup) apple sauce
2 tablespoons chicken stock
125 ml (4 fl oz/$\frac{1}{2}$ cup) pouring (whipping) cream
1 teaspoon cornflour (cornstarch)

GLAZED APPLES
2 green apples
50 g (1$\frac{3}{4}$ oz) butter
2 tablespoons soft brown sugar

SERVES 4

Preheat the oven to 180°C (350°F/Gas 4). Trim the pork fillet, removing any fat or sinew from the outside. Tie the fillet with kitchen string at 3 cm (1$\frac{1}{4}$ inch) intervals to keep in shape.

Heat the butter and oil in a frying pan, add the pork fillet and cook until lightly browned all over. Remove and place on a rack in a baking dish. (Retain the cooking oils in the frying pan.) Add 125 ml (4 fl oz/$\frac{1}{2}$ cup) water to the baking dish and bake for 15–20 minutes. Leave in a warm place for 10 minutes before removing the string and slicing.

For the sauce, reheat the oils in the frying pan, add the garlic and ginger and stir for 1 minute. Stir in the mustard, apple sauce and stock. Slowly stir in the combined cream and cornflour and stir until the mixture boils and thickens.

For the glazed apples, cut the apples into 1 cm ($\frac{1}{2}$ inch) slices. Melt the butter in the pan and add the sugar. Stir until the sugar dissolves. Add the apple slices and pan-fry, turning occasionally, until the apples are glazed and lightly browned.

Slice the pork and serve the apple and mustard sauce over it. Serve with the glazed apples.

PREPARATION TIME: 30 MINUTES   COOKING TIME: 25 MINUTES

NOTE: Pork fillets can be thick and short or long and thin and the time they take to cook will vary accordingly.

Roast pork fillet with apple and mustard sauce and glazed apples

SALMON STEAKS WITH HERB SAUCE

4 salmon steaks (250 g/9 oz each)
2 tablespoons oil

HERB SAUCE
375 ml (13 fl oz/1½ cups) fish stock
125 ml (4 fl oz/½ cup) white wine
3 tablespoons chopped chives
3 tablespoons chopped flat-leaf
(Italian) parsley
2 tablespoons chopped basil
2 tablespoons chopped tarragon
250 ml (9 fl oz/1 cup) pouring (whipping)
cream
2 egg yolks

SERVES 4

To make the herb sauce, combine the stock and wine in a saucepan and bring to the boil. Boil for 5 minutes or until the liquid has reduced by half. Transfer to a food processor, add the chives, parsley, basil and tarragon and process for 30 seconds. Return to the pan, then stir in the cream and bring to the boil. Reduce the heat to low and simmer for 5 minutes, or until reduced by half. Place the egg yolks in a food processor and process until smooth. Drizzle in the herb mixture. Process until smooth. Season.

Heat the oil in a frying pan, add the salmon steaks and cook over medium heat for 3 minutes each side, or until just cooked through. Serve hot with herb sauce.

PREPARATION TIME: 25 MINUTES   COOKING TIME: 20 MINUTES

BAKED VEAL WITH SPICY CHICKEN STUFFING

1.8 kg (4 lb) shoulder of veal, boned and
butterflied
1 tablespoon olive oil

SPICY STUFFING
2 teaspoons olive oil
6 spring onions (scallions), finely chopped
500 g (1 lb 2 oz) minced (ground) chicken
80 g (2¾ oz/1 cup) fresh wholemeal
(whole-wheat) breadcrumbs
1 teaspoon freshly grated ginger
2 red chillies, seeded and chopped
2 eggs, lightly beaten
40 g (1½ oz/⅓ cup) chopped pecans
½ teaspoon ground black pepper
¼ teaspoon paprika
½ teaspoon ground coriander

SERVES 6

Preheat the oven to 180°C (350°F/Gas 4). Trim the veal of excess fat and sinew. Place the veal, flesh side up, on a board. To make the stuffing, heat the oil in a frying pan over medium heat. Add the onion and chicken and cook for 4 minutes. Remove from the heat and add the remaining stuffing ingredients. Stir to combine. Place in a food processor and process until smooth.

Spread the stuffing over the veal, then roll up and tie with kitchen string. Brush with the olive oil and season. Place on a rack in a baking dish. Pour 375 ml (13 fl oz/1½ cups) water into the baking dish. Bake for 1½ hours for medium, or until cooked to your liking. Add extra water to the pan as necessary and skim fat from the surface. Remove the veal from the dish, cover and set aside for 10 minutes. Remove the string and carve.

Drain any excess fat from the pan juices and boil the juices on the stovetop for 2–5 minutes, or until reduced by about half. Strain, then season, to taste, and serve with the sliced veal.

PREPARATION TIME: 15 MINUTES   COOKING TIME: 1 HOUR 40 MINUTES

Salmon steaks with herb sauce

CHICKEN BALLOTTINE

1.6 kg (3 lb 8 oz) chicken
2 red capsicums (peppers)
1 kg (2 lb 4 oz) silverbeet (Swiss chard)
30 g (1 oz) butter
1 onion, finely chopped
1 garlic clove, crushed
50 g (1¾ oz/½ cup) grated parmesan cheese
80 g (2¾ oz/1 cup) fresh breadcrumbs
1 tablespoon chopped oregano
200 g (7 oz) ricotta cheese

SERVES 8

To bone the chicken, cut through the skin on the centre back with a sharp knife. Separate the flesh from the bone down one side to the breast, being careful not to pierce the skin. Follow along the bones closely with the knife, gradually easing the meat from the thigh, drumstick and wing. Cut through the thigh bone where it meets the drumstick and cut off the wing tip. Repeat on the other side, then lift the rib cage away, leaving the flesh in one piece and the drumsticks still attached to the flesh. Scrape all the meat from the drumstick and wings, discarding the bones. Turn the wing and drumstick flesh inside the chicken and lay the chicken out flat, skin side down. Refrigerate.

Preheat the oven to 180°C (350°F/Gas 4). Cut the capsicums into large flattish pieces, discarding the membranes and seeds. Cook, skin side up, under a hot grill (broiler) until the skins blister and blacken. Cool in a plastic bag, then peel.

Discard the stalks from the silverbeet and finely shred the leaves. Melt the butter in a large frying pan and cook the onion and garlic over medium heat for 5 minutes, or until soft. Add the silverbeet and stir until wilted and all the moisture has evaporated. Cool. In a food processor, process the silverbeet and onion mixture with the parmesan, breadcrumbs, oregano and half the ricotta. Season with salt and pepper.

Spread the silverbeet mixture over the chicken and lay the pepper pieces over the top. Form the remaining ricotta into a roll and place across the width of the chicken. Fold the sides of the chicken in and over the filling so they overlap slightly. Tuck the ends in neatly. Secure with toothpicks, then tie with string at 3 cm (1¼ inch) intervals.

Grease a large piece of foil and place the chicken in the centre. Roll the chicken up securely in the foil, sealing the ends well. Bake on a baking tray for 1¼–1½ hours, or until the juices run clear when a skewer is inserted in the centre of the meat. Cool, then refrigerate until cold before removing the foil, toothpicks and string. Cut into 1 cm (½ inch) slices to serve.

PREPARATION TIME: 40 MINUTES   COOKING TIME: 1 HOUR 45 MINUTES

Chicken ballottine

ROAST SIRLOIN WITH MUSTARD SAUCE

1.5 kg (3 lb 5 oz) beef sirloin
90 g (3¼ oz/⅓ cup) wholegrain mustard
1 tablespoon dijon mustard
1 teaspoon honey
1 garlic clove, crushed
1 tablespoon oil

MUSTARD SAUCE
250 ml (9 fl oz/1 cup) white wine
1 tablespoon dijon mustard
60 g (2¼ oz/¼ cup) wholegrain mustard
2 tablespoons honey
200 g (7 oz) chilled butter, cubed

SERVES 6

Preheat the oven to 220°C (425°F/Gas 7). Cut most of the fat from the piece of beef sirloin, leaving a thin layer. Mix together the mustards and add the honey and garlic. Spread over the sirloin in a thick layer. Place the oil in a baking dish and heat it in the oven for 2 minutes. Place the meat in the hot dish and roast for 15 minutes. Reduce the oven to 200°C (400°F/Gas 6) and cook for 45-50 minutes for medium-rare, or until cooked to your liking.

To make the sauce, pour the wine into a saucepan and cook over high heat for 5 minutes, or until reduced by half. Add the mustards and honey. Reduce the heat and whisk in the butter. Remove from the heat and season. Serve thin slices of the meat with the sauce and roast vegetables.

PREPARATION TIME: 15 MINUTES   COOKING TIME: 1 HOUR 30 MINUTES

TURKEY BUFFE WITH RICE AND FRUIT STUFFING

2.8 kg (6 lb) turkey buffe

STUFFING
280 g (10 oz/1½ cups) cooked rice
40 g (1½ oz/¼ cup) pine nuts, toasted
180 g (6 oz/1 cup) dried apricots, chopped
250 g (9 oz/1 cup) chopped pitted prunes
4 spring onions (scallions), sliced
1 tablespoon finely grated orange zest
80 ml (2½ fl oz/⅓ cup) orange juice
1 egg, lightly beaten

GLAZE
125 ml (4 fl oz/½ cup) orange juice
15 g (½ oz) butter
2 teaspoons soft brown sugar

SERVES 6-8

Bone the turkey breast and remove the bone from the wings.

To make the stuffing, combine the rice, pine nuts, apricots, prunes, spring onion, orange zest, juice and season. Stir in the egg.

Lay the turkey flat and spread the stuffing along the centre. Fold the breast inwards and sew the turkey together using a trussing needle and kitchen string. Tuck in the skin at the neck and press the wings in towards the breast. Tie with string. Preheat the oven to 180°C (350°F/Gas 4).

To make the glaze, stir the orange juice, butter and sugar in a saucepan. Bring to the boil and stir until the sugar is dissolved. Allow to cool.

Put the turkey on a rack in a baking dish. Bake for 1¾-2 hours, basting with the glaze. Remove from the oven, cover and set aside for 20 minutes. Remove the string or skewers. Slice and serve with the glaze.

PREPARATION TIME: 1 HOUR   COOKING TIME: 2 HOURS 10 MINUTES

POACHED OCEAN TROUT

2 litres (70 fl oz/8 cups) white wine
60 ml (2 fl oz/¼ cup) white wine vinegar
2 onions
10 cloves
4 carrots, chopped
1 lemon, cut in quarters
2 bay leaves
4 stalks flat-leaf (Italian) parsley
1 teaspoon whole black peppercorns
2.5 kg (5 lb 8 oz) ocean trout, cleaned,
gutted and scaled

DILL MAYONNAISE
1 egg, at room temperature
1 egg yolk, at room temperature
1 tablespoon lemon juice
1 teaspoon white wine vinegar
375 ml (13 fl oz/1½ cups) light olive oil
1–2 tablespoons chopped dill

SERVES 8–10

Combine the wine and vinegar with 2.5 litres (87 fl oz/10 cups) water in a large heavy-based saucepan.

Stud the onions with the cloves. Add to the pan with the carrot, lemon, bay leaves, parsley and peppercorns. Bring to the boil, reduce the heat and simmer for 30–35 minutes. Cool. Strain into a fish kettle that will hold the trout.

Place the whole fish in the fish kettle and add water if necessary, to just cover the fish. Bring to the boil, then reduce the heat to a low simmer, cover and poach gently for 10–15 minutes, until the fish flakes when tested in the thickest part. Remove the kettle from the heat and leave the fish to cool in the liquid.

For the dill mayonnaise, process the egg, yolk, lemon juice and wine vinegar in a food processor for 10 seconds, or until blended. With the motor running, add the oil in a thin, steady stream, blending until all the oil is added and the mayonnaise is thick and creamy — it should be thick enough to form peaks. Transfer to a bowl and stir in the dill and salt and pepper, to taste.

Remove the cold fish from the liquid, place on a serving platter and peel back the skin. Garnish with watercress and lemon slices. Serve with the dill mayonnaise.

PREPARATION TIME: 50 MINUTES   COOKING TIME: 50 MINUTES

NOTE: Atlantic salmon, snapper, sea bass or red emperor can also be used. If you don't have a fish kettle, use a baking dish big enough to hold the fish, cover and bake in a 180°C (350°F/Gas 4) oven for 20–30 minutes.

ROAST DUCK

2 kg (4 lb 8 oz) duck, with neck
2 chicken wings, chopped
125 ml (4 fl oz/^{1}/$_2$ cup) white wine
1 onion, chopped
1 carrot, sliced
1 ripe tomato, chopped
1 bouquet garni

ORANGE SAUCE
2 tablespoons shredded orange zest
170 ml (5^1/$_2$ fl oz/^{2}/$_3$ cup) orange juice
80 ml (2^1/$_2$ fl oz/^{1}/$_3$ cup) Cointreau
2 teaspoons cornflour (cornstarch)

SERVES 4

Place the duck neck, chicken wings and wine in a saucepan. Boil over high heat for 5 minutes, or until the wine has reduced by half. Add the onion, carrot, tomato, bouquet garni and 500 ml (17 fl oz/2 cups) water. Bring to the boil and simmer gently for 40 minutes. Strain and set aside 250 ml (9 fl oz/1 cup) of the stock.

Preheat the oven to 180°C (350°F/Gas 4). Place the duck in a saucepan, cover with boiling water, then drain. Dry with paper towels. Prick the skin of the duck with a skewer. Place the duck, breast side down, on a rack in a baking dish and bake for 50 minutes. Drain off any fat, turn the duck over and pour the reserved stock into the pan. Bake for 40 minutes, or until the breast is golden brown. Remove the duck from the pan and rest for 15 minutes before carving. Reserve the pan juices.

To make the orange sauce, skim any fat off the reserved pan juices. Place in a saucepan with the zest, juice and Cointreau and bring to the boil. Reduce the heat and simmer for 5 minutes. Blend the cornflour with 1 tablespoon water, add to the sauce and stir until the mixture thickens.

PREPARATION TIME: 40 MINUTES   COOKING TIME: 2 HOURS 15 MINUTES

LAMB CROWN ROAST WITH SAGE STUFFING

1 crown roast of lamb (12 cutlets)
20 g (^{3}/$_4$ oz) butter
2 onions, chopped
1 green apple, peeled and chopped
160 g (5^1/$_2$ oz/2 cups) fresh breadcrumbs
2 tablespoons chopped sage
1 tablespoon chopped flat-leaf (Italian) parsley
60 ml (2 fl oz/^{1}/$_4$ cup) unsweetened apple juice
2 eggs, separated

SERVES 4–6

Preheat the oven to 210°C (415°F/Gas 6-7). Trim the meat of excess fat and sinew.

Melt the butter in a saucepan. Add the onion and apple and cook over medium heat until soft. Remove from the heat and stir into the combined breadcrumbs, sage and parsley. Whisk the apple juice and egg yolks together, then stir into the breadcrumb mixture. Beat the egg whites using electric beaters until soft peaks form. Fold into the stuffing mixture.

Place the roast on a sheet of greased foil in a baking dish. Wrap some foil around the tops of the bones to prevent burning. Spoon the stuffing into the cavity. Roast for 45 minutes for medium, or until cooked to your liking. Leave for 10 minutes before cutting between the cutlets.

PREPARATION TIME: 30 MINUTES   COOKING TIME: 50 MINUTES

PORK WITH APPLE AND PRUNE STUFFING

1 green apple, chopped
90 g (3¼ oz/⅓ cup) pitted prunes,
chopped
2 tablespoons port
1 tablespoon chopped flat-leaf
(Italian) parsley
2 kg (4 lb 8 oz) piece boned pork loin
olive oil and salt, to rub on pork

GRAVY WITH WINE
2 tablespoons plain (all-purpose) flour
2 teaspoons worcestershire sauce
2 tablespoons red or white wine
560 ml (19¼ fl oz/2¼ cups) beef or
chicken stock

SERVES 8

Preheat the oven to 240°C (475°F/Gas 8). To make the stuffing, combine the apple, prune, port and parsley. Lay the pork loin on a board with the rind underneath. Spread the stuffing over the meat side of the loin, roll up and secure with skewers or string at regular intervals. If some of the filling falls out while tying, carefully push it back in. Score the pork rind with a sharp knife at 1 cm (½ inch) intervals (if the butcher hasn't already done so) and rub generously with oil and salt.

Place on a rack in a baking dish. Bake for 15 minutes, then reduce the heat to 180°C (350°F/Gas 4) and bake for 1½–2 hours, or until the pork is cooked through. The juices will run clear when a skewer is inserted into the thickest part of the meat. Cover and stand for 15 minutes before removing the skewers or string and carving. Reserve any pan juices for making the gravy.

To make the gravy, discard all but 2 tablespoons of the pan juices from the baking dish the roast was cooked in. Heat the dish on the stovetop over medium heat, stir in the flour and cook, stirring, until well browned. Remove from the heat and gradually add the worcestershire sauce, wine and stock. Return to the heat. Stir until the mixture boils and thickens, then simmer for 2 minutes. Season with salt and pepper, to taste.

PREPARATION TIME: 35 MINUTES   COOKING TIME: 2 HOURS

NOTE: If the rind fails to crackle, carefully remove it from the meat, cutting between the fat layer and the meat. Scrape off any excess fat and put the rind on a piece of foil. Place under a hot grill (broiler), and grill until the rind has crackled. Alternatively, place between several sheets of paper towel and microwave on high in 1 minute bursts, for about 2–3 minutes altogether (depending on the thickness of the rind).

STUFFED LEG OF LAMB

STUFFING

1 thick slice white bread, crusts removed

70 g (2½ oz) chicken livers, trimmed

60 g (2¼ oz) tocino or bacon

1 tablespoon dry sherry

1 garlic clove, crushed

1 tablespoon chopped flat-leaf
(Italian) parsley

½ tablespoon chopped chives

1 teaspoon finely chopped rosemary

1 tablespoon capers, finely chopped

1 large leg of lamb (3 kg/6 lb 12 oz), boned

1 teaspoon sweet paprika

1 tablespoon plain (all-purpose) flour

4 garlic cloves, peeled

2 tablespoons olive oil

375 ml (13 fl oz/1½ cups) dry white wine

1 tablespoon lard

125 ml (4 fl oz/½ cup) chicken stock

SERVES 6–8

To make the stuffing, break the bread into pieces and process with the chicken livers and tocino until medium-fine. Put in a bowl with the sherry, garlic, parsley, chives, rosemary and capers. Season and mix well.

Preheat the oven to 210°C (415°F/Gas 6–7). Lay the lamb out flat and put the filling down the centre. Roll the meat up to encase the filling. Tie with kitchen string. Combine the paprika and flour with ¼ teaspoon salt and rub all over the lamb. Put the garlic in a row in the centre of a baking dish and pour the oil over the top. Put the lamb on the garlic and pour the wine over the top. Spread the lard over the surface.

Bake for 20 minutes, then reduce the heat to 170°C (325°F/Gas 3). Baste, then bake for a further 1 hour 45 minutes, basting frequently, until the lamb is well cooked. Transfer to a carving tray and keep warm. Spoon off excess oil from the pan juices, then transfer the contents of the baking dish to a saucepan; there will be about 125 ml (4 fl oz/½ cup). Add the stock and cook over high heat until slightly thickened. Slice the lamb and arrange on a serving platter. Pour the sauce over the lamb.

PREPARATION TIME: 25 MINUTES   COOKING TIME: 2 HOURS 15 MINUTES

SPICY BAKED FISH WITH VEGETABLES

1 tablespoon ground cumin

4 garlic cloves

1 small fresh red chilli

90 g (3¼ oz) coriander (cilantro) leaves, chopped

1 teaspoon salt

1 tablespoon lemon juice

100 ml (3½ fl oz) olive oil

2 x 750 g (1 lb 10 oz) fish, such as snapper or ocean perch, scaled and cleaned

2–3 ripe tomatoes, halved, thickly sliced

450 g (1 lb) all-purpose potatoes, sliced

100 g (3½ oz) pitted green olives, halved

SERVES 4

Mix the cumin, garlic, chilli, coriander, salt and lemon juice in a food processor, to form a smooth paste. With the motor running, add 2 tablespoons of the olive oil, in a thin steady stream.

Make 3–4 shallow diagonal slits on both sides of the fish, then rub the spice mixture all over the fish. Put the fish on a plate, then cover with plastic wrap and marinate in the refrigerator for 30 minutes.

Preheat the oven to 240°C (475°F/Gas 8). Put the fish in a baking dish. Scatter the tomato, potato and olives around the fish. Pour 60 ml (2 fl oz/¼ cup) water and the remaining olive oil over the fish and vegetables. Bake, basting with the pan juices, for 40 minutes, or until cooked through. When cooked, the fish will flake apart easily when tested with a fork.

PREPARATION TIME: 15 MINUTES +   COOKING TIME: 45 MINUTES

SALMON PIE

60 g (2¼ oz) butter
1 onion, finely chopped
200 g (7 oz) button mushrooms, sliced
2 tablespoons lemon juice
200 g (7 oz) cooked poached salmon
fillet, broken into small pieces, or
220 g (7 oz) tinned red salmon
2 hard-boiled eggs, chopped
2 tablespoons chopped dill
3 tablespoons chopped flat-leaf
(Italian) parsley
185 g (6½ oz/1 cup) cooked long-grain
brown rice
60 ml (2 fl oz/¼ cup) pouring (whipping)
cream
375 g (13 oz) packet frozen puff pastry
1 egg, lightly beaten
sour cream, to serve (optional)

SERVES 4–6

Melt half the butter in a frying pan and cook the onion for 5 minutes until soft but not brown. Add the mushroom and cook for 5 minutes. Stir in the juice, then remove from the pan.

Melt the remaining butter in the pan, add the salmon and stir for 2 minutes. Remove from the heat, cool slightly and add the egg, dill, parsley, and salt and pepper, to taste. Mix gently and set aside. Mix the rice and cream in a small bowl.

Roll out half the pastry to 15 x 25 cm (6 x 10 inches). Trim the pastry neatly, saving the trimmings, and put on a greased baking tray.

Layer the filling onto the pastry, leaving a 3 cm (1¼ inch) border. Put half the rice into the centre of the pastry, then the salmon and egg mixture, followed by the mushroom, then the remaining rice. Brush the border with egg.

Roll out the other pastry half to 20 x 30 cm (8 x 12 inches) and place over the filling. Seal the edges. Make two slits in the top. Decorate with the trimmings and chill for 30 minutes.

Preheat the oven to 200°C (400°F/Gas 6). Brush the pie with egg and bake for 15 minutes. Reduce the oven to 180°C (350°F/Gas 4) and bake the pie for 25–30 minutes, or until crisp and golden. Serve with sour cream.

PREPARATION TIME: 25 MINUTES   COOKING TIME: 1 HOUR

NOTE: You will need to cook about 100 g (3½ oz/½ cup) brown rice for this recipe.

Salmon pie

DRESSED CRAB

1 kg (2 lb 4 oz) live mud crab
2–3 teaspoons lemon juice
1½ tablespoons whole-egg mayonnaise
80 g (2¾ oz/1 cup) fresh breadcrumbs
1 teaspoon worcestershire sauce
2 hard-boiled eggs
2 tablespoons chopped flat-leaf
(Italian) parsley
1 tablespoon chopped chives

SERVES 1–2

Freeze the crab for about 1 hour to immobilize it, then drop it into a saucepan of boiling water. Reduce the heat and simmer for 10 minutes, or until orange all over. Drain and cool. Twist the claws off the crab. Pull back the flap on the underside of the crab and prise off the top shell. Scrape out any creamy brown meat and set aside. Wash and dry the top shell and set aside. Remove the intestines and grey feathery gills from the main body and discard. Scrape out any remaining creamy brown meat and add to the rest.

Cut the crab in half and remove the white meat. Crack the claws and remove any meat. Chop the brown meat and combine with the lemon juice, mayonnaise and enough of the breadcrumbs to combine. Add the worcestershire sauce and salt and pepper, to taste. Press the egg yolks and whites separately through a sieve. Place the white crab meat inside the dry crab shell, on both the outside edges. Spoon the brown meat mixture into the centre of the shell and arrange the combined parsley and chives, sieved yolks and whites in rows over the brown crab meat.

PREPARATION TIME: 40 MINUTES +   COOKING TIME: 15 MINUTES

CHICKEN AND LEEK PIE

50 g (1¾ oz) butter
2 large leeks, white part only, finely sliced
4 spring onions (scallions), sliced
1 garlic clove, crushed
30 g (1 oz/¼ cup) plain (all-purpose) flour
375 ml (13 fl oz/1½ cups) chicken stock
125 ml (4 fl oz/½ cup) pouring (whipping)
cream
280 g (10 oz/2 cups) chopped
cooked chicken
2 sheets frozen puff pastry, thawed
60 ml (2 fl oz/¼ cup) milk

SERVES 4

Melt the butter in a saucepan and add the leek, spring onion and garlic. Cook over low heat for 6 minutes, or until the leek is soft. Stir in the flour and cook for 1 minute, or until foaming. Remove from the heat and stir in the stock. Return to the heat and stir until the sauce boils and thickens. Stir in the cream and chicken, then spoon into a shallow 20 cm (8 inch) pie dish and set aside to cool. Preheat the oven to 200°C (400°F/Gas 6).

Brush around the rim of the pie dish with a little milk. Put one sheet of pastry on top and seal around the edge firmly. Trim off any overhanging pastry and decorate the edge with the back of a fork. Cut the other sheet into 1 cm (½ inch) strips and roll each strip up. Arrange the spirals on top of the pie, leaving a gap between each one. Make a few holes between the spirals to let out steam, and brush the top of the pie with milk. Bake for 25–30 minutes, or until the top is golden.

PREPARATION TIME: 20 MINUTES   COOKING TIME: 40 MINUTES

ROAST CHICKEN STUFFED WITH PINE NUTS AND RICE

STUFFING

60 g (2¼ oz) clarified butter
or ghee, melted
1 onion, chopped
1 teaspoon ground allspice
60 g (2¼ oz/⅓ cup) basmati rice
30 g (1 oz/¼ cup) walnuts, chopped
50 g (1¾ oz/⅓ cup) pine nuts
55 g (2 oz/⅓ cup) sultanas (golden raisins)
125 ml (4 fl oz/½ cup) chicken stock

1.6 kg (3 lb 8 oz) chicken
170 ml (5½ fl oz/⅔ cup) chicken stock

SERVES 4–6

Preheat the oven to 180°C (350°F/Gas 4). Pour half the butter into a large frying pan, then add the onion and cook for 5 minutes over medium heat until the onion is transparent. Stir in the allspice.

Add the rice and nuts to the pan, then cook for 3–4 minutes over medium-high heat. Add the sultanas, stock and 60 ml (2 fl oz/¼ cup) of water. Bring to boil, then reduce the heat and simmer for 8–10 minutes, until the water is absorbed. Allow to cool.

Rinse the cavity of the chicken with cold water and pat dry inside and out with paper towels.

When the stuffing is cool, spoon the stuffing into the cavity. Truss the chicken, using string, then place in a deep baking dish, then rub ½ teaspoon salt and ¼ teaspoon freshly ground black pepper into the skin, using your fingertips.

Pour the remainder of the butter over the chicken, then add the stock to the pan. Roast for 2 hours 10 minutes, basting every 20–25 minutes with juices from the pan. Rest the chicken for 15 minutes before carving. Serve with the stuffing.

PREPARATION TIME: 30 MINUTES   COOKING TIME: 2 HOURS 30 MINUTES

Roast chicken stuffed with pine nuts and rice

ROAST BEEF WITH YORKSHIRE PUDDINGS

2 kg (4 lb 8 oz) piece roasting beef (scotch fillet, rump or sirloin)
2 garlic cloves, crushed

YORKSHIRE PUDDINGS
90 g (3¼ oz/¾ cup) plain (all-purpose) flour
125 ml (4 fl oz/½ cup) milk
2 eggs

RED WINE GRAVY
2 tablespoons plain (all-purpose) flour
80 ml (2½ fl oz/⅓ cup) red wine
600 ml (21 fl oz) beef stock

SERVES 6

Preheat the oven to 240°C (475°F/Gas 9). Rub the piece of beef with the crushed garlic and some freshly cracked black pepper and drizzle with oil. Bake on a rack in a baking dish for 20 minutes.

To make the Yorkshire puddings, sift the flour and ½ teaspoon salt into a large bowl, then make a well in the centre and whisk in the milk. In a separate bowl, whisk the eggs together until fluffy, then add to the batter and mix well. Add 125 ml (4 fl oz/½ cup) water and whisk until large bubbles form on the surface. Cover the bowl with plastic wrap and refrigerate for 1 hour.

Reduce the oven to 180°C (350°F/Gas 4) and continue to roast the meat for 1 hour for rare, or longer for well done. Cover loosely with foil and leave in a warm place while making the Yorkshire puddings.

Increase the oven to 220°C (425°F/Gas 7). Pour off all the pan juices into a jug and spoon ½ teaspoon of the juices into twelve 80 ml (2½ fl oz/⅓ cup) patty or muffin tins. (Reserve the remaining juice for the gravy.) Heat the muffin tins in the oven until the fat is almost smoking. Whisk the batter again until bubbles form on the surface. Pour into each muffin tin to three-quarters full. Bake for 20 minutes, or until puffed and lightly golden. Make the gravy while the Yorkshire puddings are baking.

To make the gravy, heat 2 tablespoons of the reserved pan juices in the baking dish on the stovetop over low heat. Add the flour and stir well, scraping the dish to incorporate all the sediment. Cook over medium heat for 1–2 minutes, stirring constantly, until the flour is well browned. Remove from the heat and gradually stir in the wine and stock. Return to the heat, stirring constantly, until the gravy boils and thickens. Simmer for 3 minutes, then season, to taste, with salt and freshly ground black pepper. Strain, if desired.

Serve the beef with the hot Yorkshire puddings and red wine gravy.

PREPARATION TIME: 15 MINUTES +   COOKING TIME: 1 HOUR 40 MINUTES

Roast beef with Yorkshire puddings

ROAST GOOSE

3 kg (6 lb 12 oz) goose

GRAVY
1 tablespoon plain (all-purpose) flour
2 tablespoons brandy
375 ml (13 fl oz/1½ cups) chicken stock

BREAD SAUCE
1 small onion, sliced
315 ml (10¾ fl oz/1¼ cups) milk
1 bay leaf
4 black peppercorns
2 whole cloves
100 g (3½ oz/1¼ cups) fresh breadcrumbs
a pinch of freshly grated nutmeg
20 g (¾ oz) butter

SERVES 6

Preheat the oven to 180°C (350°F/Gas 4). Remove any excess fat from inside the cavity of the goose. Put the goose in a large pan, cover with boiling water, then drain. Dry with paper towels. Put the goose, breast side down, on a rack in a very large baking dish. Using a fine skewer, prick the skin of the goose all over. Bake for 1 hour, then remove from the oven and drain off any excess fat. Turn the goose over and bake for a further 30 minutes, or until golden. Remove from the baking dish, cover with foil and leave for 5–10 minutes.

To make the gravy, drain all except 2 tablespoons of fat from the baking dish and put the dish on the stovetop over low heat. Add the flour and stir over medium heat until well browned. Gradually stir in the brandy and chicken stock. Stir until the gravy boils and thickens. Season.

To make the sauce, combine the onion, milk, bay leaf, peppercorns and cloves in a saucepan. Bring to the boil over medium heat, then reduce the heat and simmer for 10 minutes. Strain into a bowl and discard the onion and flavourings. Add the breadcrumbs, nutmeg and butter. Stir, then season.

PREPARATION TIME: 15 MINUTES   COOKING TIME: 1 HOUR 30 MINUTES

LOBSTER THERMIDOR

1 cooked lobster
80 g (2¾ oz) butter
4 spring onions (scallions), finely chopped
2 tablespoons plain (all-purpose) flour
½ teaspoon dry mustard
2 tablespoons white wine or sherry
250 ml (9 fl oz/1 cup) milk
60 ml (2 fl oz/¼ cup) pouring (whipping) cream
1 tablespoon chopped flat-leaf (Italian) parsley
60 g (2¼ oz) gruyère cheese, grated

SERVES 2

Using a knife, cut the lobster in half lengthways through the shell. Lift the meat from the tail and body. Remove the cream-coloured vein and soft body matter and discard. Cut the meat into 2 cm (¾ inch) pieces, cover and refrigerate. Wash the head and shell halves, then drain and pat dry.

In a frying pan, heat 60 g (2¼ oz) of the butter, add the spring onion and stir for 2 minutes. Stir in the flour and mustard and cook for 1 minute, or until foaming. Add the wine and milk and stir until the mixture thickens. Reduce the heat and simmer for 1 minute. Stir in the cream, parsley and lobster meat, then season. Stir over low heat until heated through. Spoon the mixture into the lobster shells, sprinkle with cheese and dot with the remaining butter. Place under the grill (broiler) for 2 minutes, or until lightly browned.

PREPARATION TIME: 25 MINUTES   COOKING TIME: 5–10 MINUTES

BARBECUED SEAFOOD PLATTER

6 Balmain bugs or slipper lobsters
30 g (1 oz) butter, melted
1 tablespoon oil
12 black mussels
12 scallops on their shells
12 oysters
18 raw large prawns (shrimp), unpeeled

SALSA VERDE

1 tablespoon chopped preserved lemon
20 g (^{3}/$_4$ oz/1 cup) flat-leaf (Italian) parsley
1 tablespoon drained bottled capers
1 tablespoon lemon juice
3 tablespoons oil

VINEGAR AND SHALLOT DRESSING

60 ml (2 fl oz/^{1}/$_4$ cup) white wine vinegar
4 French shallots, finely chopped
1 tablespoon chopped chervil

PICKLED GINGER AND WASABI SAUCE

1 teaspoon soy sauce
60 ml (2 fl oz/^{1}/$_4$ cup) mirin
2 tablespoons rice wine vinegar
^{1}/$_4$ teaspoon wasabi paste
2 tablespoons finely sliced pickled ginger

SWEET BALSAMIC DRESSING

1 tablespoon olive oil
1 tablespoon honey
125 ml (4 fl oz/^{1}/$_2$ cup) balsamic vinegar

THAI CORIANDER SAUCE

125 ml (4 fl oz/^{1}/$_2$ cup) sweet chilli sauce
1 tablespoon lime juice
2 tablespoons chopped coriander (cilantro)

SERVES 6

Freeze the bugs for 1 hour to immobilize. Cut each bug in half with a sharp knife, then brush the flesh with the combined butter and oil. Set aside while you prepare the rest of the seafood.

Scrub the mussels with a stiff brush and pull out the hairy beards. Discard any broken mussels, or open ones that don't close when tapped on the bench. Rinse well.

Pull off any vein, membrane or hard white muscle from the scallops, leaving any roe attached. Brush the scallops with the combined butter and oil. Cook them, shell side down, on the barbecue.

Remove the oysters from the shells, then rinse the shells under cold water. Pat the shells dry and return the oysters to their shells. Cover and refrigerate all the seafood while you make the dressings.

To make the salsa verde, combine all the ingredients in a food processor and process in short bursts until chopped. Transfer to a bowl and add enough oil to moisten the mixture. Season. Serve a dollop on each scallop.

To make the vinegar and shallot dressing, whisk the vinegar, shallot and chervil in a bowl until combined. Pour over the cooked mussels.

To make the pickled ginger and wasabi sauce, whisk all the ingredients in a bowl until combined. Spoon over the cooked oysters.

To make the sweet balsamic dressing, heat the oil in a pan, add the honey and vinegar and bring to the boil, then boil until reduced by half. Drizzle over the cooked bugs.

To make the Thai coriander sauce, combine all the ingredients in a jug or bowl and drizzle over the cooked prawns.

Cook the seafood on a preheated barbecue grill and flatplate. The mussels, scallops, oysters and prawns all take about 2–5 minutes to cook. The bugs are cooked when the flesh turns white and starts to come away from the shells.

PREPARATION TIME: 40 MINUTES +   COOKING TIME: 30 MINUTES

SIDES AND SALADS

HASSELBACK POTATOES

8 all-purpose potatoes (such as spunta, sebago, russet, desiree, pontiac)
20 g (^{3}/4 oz) butter, melted
2 teaspoons dry breadcrumbs
2 teaspoons grated parmesan cheese (optional)

SERVES 4

Preheat the oven to 180°C (350°F/Gas 4). Cut a slice off the base of each potato so the potato will sit flat. Place, cut side down, on a board and make thin evenly spaced cuts about two-thirds of the way through each potato.

Put on a lightly greased baking dish. Brush the potatoes with butter, then sprinkle with a mixture of the breadcrumbs and parmesan. Roast for 40–50 minutes, or until golden brown and tender.

PREPARATION TIME: 20 MINUTES   COOKING TIME: 50 MINUTES

MINTED PEAS

620 g (1 lb 6 oz/4 cups) fresh or
frozen peas

4 sprigs mint

30 g (1 oz) butter

2 tablespoons shredded mint

SERVES 6

Put the peas in a saucepan and pour in water to just cover the peas. Add the mint sprigs.

Bring to the boil and simmer for 5 minutes (only 2 minutes if frozen), or until the peas are just tender. Drain and discard the mint. Return to the saucepan, add the butter and shredded mint and stir over low heat until the butter has melted. Season with salt and cracked pepper.

PREPARATION TIME: 5 MINUTES   COOKING TIME: 6 MINUTES

HONEY-ROASTED VEGETABLES

4 parsnips

2 carrots

2 small orange sweet potatoes

4 beetroot (beets), cut into wedges

8 garlic cloves, unpeeled

60 ml (2 fl oz/¼ cup) oil

1 tablespoon honey

1 teaspoon cumin seeds

SERVES 4

Preheat the oven to 200°C (400°F/Gas 6). Cut the parsnips, carrots and sweet potatoes into 10 cm (4 inch) lengths. Place the vegetables and the unpeeled garlic in a large baking dish, and drizzle with the oil and honey. Sprinkle with the cumin seeds, pepper and salt. Toss to coat.

Bake the vegetables for 40-50 minutes, or until tender inside and golden brown outside. Season with salt and cracked pepper.

PREPARATION TIME: 20 MINUTES   COOKING TIME: 50 MINUTES

RISOTTO-STUFFED ONIONS

8 onions (about 200 g/7 oz each)
1 tablespoon oil
20 g (^{3}/$_4$ oz) butter
70 g (2^1/$_4$ oz) mushrooms, chopped
20 g (^{3}/$_4$ oz) prosciutto, chopped
110 g (3^3/$_4$ oz/^{1}/$_2$ cup) risotto rice
625 ml (21^1/$_2$ fl oz/2^1/$_2$ cups) hot chicken stock
2 tablespoons grated parmesan cheese
2 tablespoons chopped flat-leaf (Italian) parsley

SERVES 8

Preheat the oven to 200°C (400°F/Gas 6). Trim the bases of the onions so they sit flat and cut the tops off, leaving a wide opening. Place in a baking dish, drizzle with the oil and bake for 1–1^1/$_2$ hours, or until golden.

Meanwhile, melt the butter in a saucepan, add the mushrooms and prosciutto and cook for 5 minutes, or until the mushrooms have softened. Add the rice and stir until well coated with the butter. Gradually stir in the hot chicken stock, about 125 ml (4 fl oz/^{1}/$_2$ cup) at a time, making sure the liquid has been absorbed before adding more. When all the stock has been absorbed, stir in the parmesan and parsley.

Scoop out the flesh from the middle of each onion, leaving at least three outside layers on each, to hold the filling. Chop the scooped flesh and stir through the risotto mixture. Spoon the filling into the onion shells, piling a little on top. Bake for 10 minutes to heat through, then serve.

PREPARATION TIME: 15 MINUTES   COOKING TIME: 1 HOUR 40 MINUTES

HERBED CARROTS

1 kg (2 lb 4 oz) carrots
40 g (1½ oz) butter
2 teaspoons sugar
2 teaspoons lemon juice
2 teaspoons finely chopped flat-leaf (Italian) parsley

SERVES 6

Peel the carrots and cut into thick matchsticks. Cook in a saucepan of boiling water for 3–5 minutes, or until tender. Drain well.

Melt the butter in the saucepan and add the sugar. Return the carrots to the saucepan and toss together until the carrots start to colour a little. Add the lemon juice and parsley and toss together until the carrots are well coated.

PREPARATION TIME: 15 MINUTES   COOKING TIME: 10 MINUTES

STEAMED MIXED BEAN BUNDLES

8 long chives
20 green beans
20 wax or yellow beans

SERVES 4

Place the chives in a small bowl. Cover with boiling water to soften, then drain.

Trim the tops and tails from all the beans, divide into eight bundles and tie them together with a chive. Place the bundles in a steamer over a saucepan half-filled with simmering water, or, alternatively, place them in a saucepan with 3 tablespoons of water.

Cover the steamer and steam the beans over medium heat for 5–8 minutes, or until just tender. Don't allow the water to completely evaporate — add more if necessary. Sprinkle the cooked beans with salt and ground black pepper and serve immediately.

PREPARATION TIME: 15 MINUTES   COOKING TIME: 8 MINUTES

ORANGE POPPY SEED ROASTED VEGETABLES

500 g (1 lb 2 oz) all-purpose potatoes, halved
6 parsnips, peeled and quartered lengthways
500 g (1 lb 2 oz) orange sweet potato, cut into large chunks
330 g (11½ oz) baby carrots, some with tops on
6 baby onions, halved
80 ml (2½ fl oz/⅓ cup) oil
2 tablespoons poppy seeds
200 g (7 oz) triple-cream brie, thinly sliced

ORANGE DRESSING
125 ml (4 fl oz/½ cup) orange juice
2 garlic cloves, crushed
1 tablespoon dijon mustard
1 teaspoon white wine vinegar
1 teaspoon sesame oil

SERVES 8

Preheat the oven to 200°C (400°F/Gas 6). Place all the vegetables and the oil in a large deep baking dish. Toss the vegetables to coat with the oil. Bake for 50 minutes, or until the vegetables are crisp and tender, tossing every 15 minutes. Remove from the oven and sprinkle with the poppy seeds.

To make the orange dressing, whisk the ingredients together in a small bowl.

Pour the dressing over the warm vegetables and toss. Transfer to a large bowl, top with the brie and serve immediately while still warm.

PREPARATION TIME: 20 MINUTES   COOKING TIME: 50 MINUTES

SPICED RED CABBAGE

750 g (1 lb 10 oz) red cabbage
1 large red onion, chopped
1 green apple, cored and chopped
2 garlic cloves, crushed
$\frac{1}{4}$ teaspoon ground cloves
$\frac{1}{4}$ teaspoon freshly grated nutmeg
1$\frac{1}{2}$ tablespoons soft brown sugar
2 tablespoons red wine vinegar
20 g ($\frac{3}{4}$ oz) butter, cubed

SERVES 6

Preheat the oven to 150°C (300°F/Gas 2). Quarter the cabbage and remove the core. Finely slice the cabbage and put it in a large ovenproof casserole dish with the onion and apple. Toss well.

Combine the garlic, spices, sugar and vinegar in a small bowl. Pour the mixture over the cabbage, and toss. Dot the top with the butter. Cover and bake for 1$\frac{1}{2}$ hours, stirring once or twice. Season to taste with salt and freshly ground black pepper. Serve hot.

PREPARATION TIME: 20 MINUTES   COOKING TIME: 1 HOUR 30 MINUTES

ROAST PUMPKIN

1 kg (2 lb 4 oz) pumpkin (winter squash)
1 tablespoon oil
20 g ($\frac{3}{4}$ oz) butter, melted
$\frac{1}{2}$ teaspoon ground paprika
$\frac{1}{2}$ teaspoon ground cumin

SERVES 4–6

Preheat the oven to 180°C (350°F/Gas 4). Cut the pumpkin into eight pieces and toss with the oil, butter, paprika and cumin. Roast in a lightly greased baking dish for 40 minutes, or until browned and tender, turning once.

PREPARATION TIME: 10 MINUTES   COOKING TIME: 40 MINUTES

Spiced red cabbage

BRUSSELS SPROUTS AND CHESTNUTS

500 g (1 lb 2 oz) fresh chestnuts or
240 g (8½ oz) tinned
1 kg (2 lb 4 oz) brussels sprouts
30 g (1 oz) butter
freshly grated nutmeg

SERVES 8

Make slits in the skins of the chestnuts and put them in a saucepan. Cover with cold water and bring to the boil over high heat. Reduce the heat and simmer for 10 minutes. Drain and leave until cool enough to handle. Peel off the skins.

Trim the sprouts and cut a cross in the base of each. Bring a saucepan of water to the boil, add the sprouts and simmer for 5–8 minutes, or until just tender. Melt the butter in a large frying pan and add the chestnuts. Cook until they begin to brown, then add the sprouts and toss together until heated through. Season well with salt, pepper and nutmeg.

PREPARATION TIME: 30 MINUTES   COOKING TIME: 20 MINUTES

ROAST ORANGE SWEET POTATO

800 g (1 lb 10 oz) orange sweet potato
20 g (3/4 oz) butter, melted
2 teaspoons sesame seeds
1/2 teaspoon cracked black pepper

SERVES 4

Preheat the oven to 180°C (350°F/Gas 4). Cut the orange sweet potato into 1 cm (1/2 inch) thick slices. Combine with the butter, sesame seeds and pepper. Toss well, then roast in a lightly greased baking dish for 25 minutes, or until lightly browned and tender, turning once. Sprinkle with salt before serving.

PREPARATION TIME: 10 MINUTES   COOKING TIME: 25 MINUTES

ROAST ONIONS

6 onions
60 g (2 1/4 oz/3/4 cup) fresh breadcrumbs
25 g (1 oz/1/4 cup) grated romano or parmesan cheese
1 tablespoon chopped basil
20 g (3/4 oz) butter, melted

SERVES 6

Preheat the oven to 180°C (350°F/Gas 4). Peel the onions, leaving the root ends intact. Put in a saucepan of water, bring to the boil and simmer gently for 20 minutes. Remove and cool. Cut off and discard the top quarter of each onion, and scoop out a third of the inside.

Combine the breadcrumbs, cheese, basil and butter in a bowl and season. Spoon into the onions and roast in a lightly greased baking dish for 50 minutes, or until the onions are soft.

PREPARATION TIME: 20 MINUTES   COOKING TIME: 1 HOUR 10 MINUTES

ROASTED STUFFED TOMATOES

6 ripe tomatoes
20 g (³/₄ oz) butter
2 bacon slices, finely chopped
75 g (2¹/₂ oz) button mushrooms,
finely chopped
1 spring onion (scallion), finely chopped
80 g (2³/₄ oz/1 cup) fresh breadcrumbs
oil, for drizzling

SERVES 6

Preheat the oven to 180°C (350°F/Gas 4). Cut the tops off the tomatoes, reserving the tops. Scoop out the seeds and soft flesh. Melt the butter over low heat and fry the bacon and button mushrooms for 5 minutes, or until soft. Transfer to a bowl. Stir in the spring onion and breadcrumbs and season with salt and freshly ground black pepper. Fill the tomatoes with the mixture and replace the tops. Place on a baking tray and drizzle with oil. Roast for 20 minutes, or until heated through.

PREPARATION TIME: 20 MINUTES   COOKING TIME: 25 MINUTES

ROAST PARSNIPS

4 parsnips, peeled
1 tablespoon olive oil
20 g (³/4 oz) butter, melted
1 tablespoon maple syrup

SERVES 4

Preheat the oven to 180°C (350°F/Gas 4). Cut off the thin part of the parsnips, then cut each thick section into quarters lengthways. Toss with the oil and butter in a baking dish and roast for 35 minutes, or until lightly browned, tossing occasionally. Drizzle the maple syrup over the parsnips and roast for 5 minutes.

PREPARATION TIME: 10 MINUTES   COOKING TIME: 40 MINUTES

ORANGE SWEET POTATO CRUMBLE

1 kg (2 lb 4 oz) orange sweet potato
50 g (1³/4 oz) butter
80 ml (2³/4 fl oz/¹/3 cup) milk
¹/4 teaspoon ground cinnamon
480 g (1 lb 1 oz) loaf sourdough bread
55 g (2 oz/¹/2 cup) grated parmesan cheese
1 teaspoon dried thyme leaves

SERVES 6

Preheat the oven to 180°C (350°F/Gas 4). Cut the orange sweet potato into chunks, put in a saucepan and cook in salted boiling water for 15 minutes, or until tender. Drain and return to the saucepan. Mash with a potato masher, adding the butter, milk and cinnamon. Season, to taste, with salt and freshly ground pepper, then spoon into a shallow 1 litre (35 fl oz/4 cup) capacity casserole dish and smooth the top.

For the crumble topping, remove the crusts from the bread, break the bread into smaller pieces and finely chop in a food processor. Mix in the parmesan and thyme, then scatter over the mash and bake for 20 minutes, or until the crumble is golden and crispy.

PREPARATION TIME: 25 MINUTES   COOKING TIME: 40 MINUTES

TOMATO AND FENNEL IN ROASTED RED CAPSICUMS

2 small fennel bulbs
3 large red capsicums (peppers)
6 ripe roma (plum) tomatoes
6 garlic cloves, sliced
3 teaspoons fennel seeds
60 ml (2 fl oz/¼ cup) lemon juice
2 tablespoons olive oil

SERVES 6

Preheat the oven to 180°C (350°F/Gas 4). Brush a large baking dish with oil.

Cut each fennel bulb in half, then cut into thick slices. Put in a saucepan of boiling salted water and cook for 1 minute. Drain and allow to cool.

Cut the capsicums in half lengthways, leaving the stalks attached. Remove the seeds and membranes.

Cut the tomatoes in half lengthways and arrange in the capsicum halves with the fennel slices. (The amount of fennel used will depend on the size of the capsicum and the fennel, but the vegetables should fit firmly inside the capsicum.) Add garlic slices to each capsicum half and sprinkle with fennel seeds. Season with salt and freshly ground black pepper. Sprinkle the lemon juice and half the oil over the capsicums.

Bake for 1 hour, or until the capsicums are tender, brushing with the remaining oil once or twice during cooking. Serve hot.

PREPARATION TIME: 20 MINUTES   COOKING TIME: 1 HOUR

PANCETTA POTATOES

8 floury or all-purpose potatoes
(such as sebago, spunta, russet,
desiree, pontiac)
2 slices pancetta
8 sprigs rosemary
10 g (¼ oz) butter, softened
oil, for brushing

SERVES 4

Preheat the oven to 180°C (350°F/Gas 4). Cut the potatoes and trim the bases so they sit flat. Cut each pancetta slice lengthways into four pieces. Roll a sprig of rosemary in each piece of pancetta. Cut a hole in the centre of the potatoes about halfway through and insert the pancetta. Place on a greased baking dish. Top each potato with ¼ teaspoon of the butter. Brush with oil and sprinkle with pepper. Roast for 40–50 minutes, or until golden.

PREPARATION TIME: 20 MINUTES   COOKING TIME: 50 MINUTES

NOTE: The texture of potatoes varies from waxy to floury or starchy and it is best to use the type stated in recipes. Sebago and pontiac are good all-rounders and are particularly good for baking. Russet and spunta have a floury texture and are also good baking varieties.

BROCCOLI WITH ALMONDS

500 g (1 lb 2 oz) broccoli, cut into
small florets
2 teaspoons oil
20 g (¾ oz) butter
1 garlic clove, crushed
1 tablespoon flaked almonds

SERVES 6

Add the broccoli to a saucepan of boiling water and cook for 1–2 minutes, or until just tender. Drain thoroughly.

Heat the oil and butter in a large frying pan, add the garlic and almonds and cook for 1–2 minutes, or until the almonds are golden. Remove from the pan and set aside.

Add the broccoli to the frying pan and toss over medium heat for 2–3 minutes, or until the broccoli is heated through. Return the almonds to the pan and stir until well distributed. Serve hot.

PREPARATION TIME: 10 MINUTES   COOKING TIME: 10 MINUTES

CREAMY POTATO GRATIN

750 g (1 lb 10 oz) waxy or
all-purpose potatoes
1 onion
125 g (4½ oz/1 cup) grated cheddar
cheese
375 ml (13 fl oz/1½ cups) pouring
(whipping) cream
2 teaspoons chicken stock
(bouillon) powder

SERVES 6

Preheat the oven to 180°C (350°F/Gas 4). Thinly slice the potatoes and slice the onion into rings.

Arrange a layer of overlapping potato slices in a baking dish and top with a layer of onion rings. Divide the cheese in half and set aside one half for topping. Sprinkle a little of the remaining cheese over the onion. Continue layering in this order until all the potato and the onion have been used, finishing with a little cheese.

Pour the cream into a small jug, add the chicken stock powder and whisk gently until thoroughly combined. Pour the mixture over the layered potato and onion and sprinkle the top with the reserved cheese. Bake for 40 minutes, or until the potato is tender, the cheese has melted and the top is golden brown.

PREPARATION TIME: 20 MINUTES   COOKING TIME: 40 MINUTES

NOTES: A gratin is any dish topped with cheese and/or breadcrumbs and cooked until browned. There are many versions of potato gratin — some are creamy like this one, others less so. If you prefer, you can use different types of stock, including vegetable, to vary the flavour. Waxy or all-purpose potatoes are best as they hold their shape better when cooked in this way. If you have a mandolin, use it to cut the potatoes into thin slices. If not, use a very sharp knife.

BRAISED FENNEL

4 small fennel bulbs
20 g (³/₄ oz) butter
1 tablespoon sugar
80 ml (2¹/₂ fl oz/¹/₃ cup) white wine
160 ml (5 fl oz/²/₃ cup) chicken stock
1 tablespoon sour cream

SERVES 8

Slice the fennel bulbs into quarters, reserving the fronds. Melt the butter in a frying pan and stir in the sugar. Add the fennel, and cook for 5–10 minutes, or until lightly browned all over.

Pour in the wine and stock and bring to the boil, then reduce the heat and simmer, covered, for 10 minutes, or until tender.

Uncover and boil until most of the liquid has evaporated and the sauce has become sticky. Remove from the heat and stir in the sour cream. Garnish with the reserved fennel fronds.

PREPARATION TIME: 15 MINUTES   COOKING TIME: 30 MINUTES

ROAST POTATOES

4 large floury or all-purpose potatoes
(such as spunta, sebago, russet,
desiree, pontiac)
20 g (³/₄ oz) butter, melted
1 tablespoon olive oil

SERVES 4

Preheat the oven to 180°C (350°F/Gas 4). Cut the potatoes in half and simmer in a saucepan of water for 5 minutes. Drain, then cool on paper towels.

Using a fork, scrape the rounded side of the potatoes to form a rough surface. Place on a greased baking dish and brush with the butter and oil. Roast for 50 minutes, or until golden, brushing halfway through the cooking time with a little more butter and oil.

PREPARATION TIME: 15 MINUTES   COOKING TIME: 55 MINUTES

ASPARAGUS WITH BUTTER AND PARMESAN

300 g (10½ oz) asparagus
40 g (1½ oz) butter, melted
parmesan cheese shavings, to serve
SERVES 4–6

Snap any thick woody ends from the asparagus and discard. Peel the bottom half of each spear with a vegetable peeler if the skin is very thick.

Plunge the asparagus into a saucepan of boiling water and cook for 2–3 minutes, or until the asparagus is bright-green and just tender. Drain and place on serving plates. Drizzle with a little melted butter. Top with parmesan shavings and sprinkle with cracked black pepper.

PREPARATION TIME: 15 MINUTES   COOKING TIME: 3 MINUTES

NOTE: You can use green, purple or white asparagus for this recipe, or a combination. Lightly toasted, crushed hazelnuts or pecan nuts can be sprinkled over the top.

Asparagus with butter and parmesan

SWEET ROAST BEETROOT

12 small fresh beetroot (beets)
1½ tablespoons olive oil
20 g (¾ oz) butter
1½ teaspoons ground cumin
1 teaspoon coriander seeds,
lightly crushed
½ teaspoon mixed (pumpkin pie) spice
1 garlic clove, crushed (optional)
3-4 teaspoons soft brown sugar
1 tablespoon balsamic vinegar

SERVES 6

Preheat the oven to 180°C (350°F/Gas 4) and brush a baking dish with melted butter or oil. Trim the leafy tops from the beetroot (cut about 3 cm/1¼ inches above the pulp to prevent bleeding), wash the bulbs thoroughly and place on the tray. Bake for 1 hour 15 minutes, or until very tender. Set aside until the bulbs are cool enough to handle.

Peel the beetroot and trim the tops and tails to neaten. Heat the oil and butter in a frying pan, add the cumin, coriander seeds, mixed spice and garlic and cook over medium heat for 1 minute. Add the sugar and vinegar to the pan and stir for 2-3 minutes, or until the sugar dissolves. Add the beetroot, reduce the heat to low and turn the beetroot for 5 minutes, or until glazed all over. Serve warm or at room temperature.

PREPARATION TIME: 15 MINUTES   COOKING TIME: 1 HOUR 30 MINUTES

CAULIFLOWER CHEESE

500 g (1 lb 2 oz) cauliflower, cut into
small pieces
2 tablespoons fresh breadcrumbs
30 g (1 oz/¼ cup) grated cheddar cheese

CHEESE SAUCE
30 g (1 oz) butter
1½ tablespoons plain (all-purpose) flour
315 ml (10¾ fl oz/1¼ cups) warm milk
1 teaspoon dijon mustard
60 g (2¼ oz/½ cup) grated
cheddar cheese
50 g (1¾ oz/½ cup) grated
parmesan cheese

SERVES 4

Lightly grease a 1.5 litre (48 fl oz/6 cup) heatproof dish. Cook the cauliflower pieces in a saucepan of lightly salted boiling water for 10 minutes, or until just tender. Drain thoroughly, then transfer to the prepared dish and keep warm.

For the cheese sauce, melt the butter in a pan over low heat. Stir in the flour and cook for 1 minute, or until pale and foaming. Remove from the heat and gradually stir in the milk and mustard. Return to the heat and stir constantly until the sauce boils and thickens. Reduce the heat and simmer for 2 minutes, then remove the pan from the heat. Add the cheddar and parmesan and stir until melted. Do not reheat or the oil will come out of the cheese. Season with salt and white pepper, to taste, and pour over the cauliflower.

Combine the breadcrumbs and cheddar and sprinkle over the sauce. Grill under medium heat until the top is brown and bubbling. Serve immediately.

PREPARATION TIME: 15 MINUTES   COOKING TIME: 20 MINUTES·

DUCHESS POTATOES

860 g (1 lb 12 oz) floury potatoes, such as russet and spunta, quartered

2 eggs

60 ml (2 fl oz/¼ cup) pouring (whipping) cream

2 tablespoons freshly grated parmesan cheese

¼ teaspoon freshly grated nutmeg

1 egg yolk, for glazing

SERVES 6

Cook the potato in a saucepan of boiling water over medium heat for 10 minutes, or until just tender (pierce with the point of a small knife — if the potato comes away easily, it is ready). Drain and return to the pan. Reduce the heat to very low and shake the pan for 1–2 minutes to dry out the potato. Transfer to a bowl and mash well until smooth.

Beat together the eggs, cream, parmesan, nutmeg and some salt and black pepper. Add to the potato and mash to combine. Season to taste. Cover and leave for 20 minutes to cool slightly. Preheat the oven to 180°C (350°F/Gas 4).

Put the just-warm potato mixture in a piping bag with a 1.5 cm (⅝ inch) star nozzle. Pipe the mixture in swirls, not too close together, onto greased baking trays. Brush lightly all over with the extra egg yolk, to give a golden, crisp finish. Bake for 15–20 minutes, or until golden. Serve hot, sprinkled with a little paprika if desired.

PREPARATION TIME: 20 MINUTES +   COOKING TIME: 30 MINUTES

ROAST VEGETABLE MASH

2 large pontiac or sebago potatoes
400 g (14 oz) pumpkin (winter squash)
400 g (14 oz) orange sweet potato
2 large parsnips
1 large onion, chopped
2 ripe tomatoes, quartered
6 garlic cloves, unpeeled
2 tablespoons olive oil
30 g (1 oz) butter, chopped

SERVES 4–6

Preheat the oven to 180°C (375°F/Gas 4). Peel the potatoes, pumpkin, orange sweet potato and parsnip, then cut into large pieces and place in a large baking dish with the onion, tomato and garlic. Drizzle with oil and sprinkle with salt and cracked black pepper.

Bake the vegetables for 1½ hours, or until soft and starting to brown, turning every 30 minutes. Peel the garlic.

Transfer the vegetables to a bowl, add the butter and mash. Season, to taste, with salt and freshly ground pepper.

PREPARATION TIME: 30 MINUTES   COOKING TIME: 1 HOUR 30 MINUTES

NOTE: You could also substitute swedes (rutabagas), celeriac or Jerusalem artichoke for the parsnips, or carrot for pumpkin or orange sweet potato. Fresh herbs are also a tasty addition — stir through some chopped basil or parsley when mashing the vegetables.

TOMATOES STUFFED WITH FETA

6 ripe tomatoes
150 g (5½ oz) crumbled Greek feta cheese
2 teaspoons chopped oregano
1 tablespoon freshly grated parmesan cheese

MAKES 6

Preheat the oven to 200°C (400°F/Gas 6). Cut a deep cross in the tops of the tomatoes. Combine the feta in a bowl with the oregano and parmesan. Season with pepper.

Stuff each tomato with about 1 tablespoon of the feta mixture. Bake for 20 minutes, or until the skins split and soften.

PREPARATION TIME: 10 MINUTES   COOKING TIME: 20 MINUTES

COLD POTATO SALAD

1.2 kg (2 lb 12 oz) waxy white or red potatoes, unpeeled and cut into bite-sized pieces
2 onions, finely chopped
2 green capsicums (peppers), chopped
4-5 celery sticks, chopped
6 tablespoons finely chopped flat-leaf (Italian) parsley

DRESSING
375 g (13 oz/1½ cups) whole-egg mayonnaise
3-4 tablespoons white wine vinegar or lemon juice
90 g (3¼ oz/⅓ cup) sour cream

SERVES 8

Steam or boil the potato for 5–10 minutes, or until just tender (pierce with the point of a small sharp knife — if the potato comes away easily it is ready). Don't let the skins break away. Drain and cool completely.

Combine the onion, capsicum, celery and parsley with the potato in a large bowl, reserving some parsley for garnish.

To make the dressing, mix together all the ingredients in a bowl and season with salt and black pepper. Pour over the salad and toss gently. Garnish with the reserved parsley.

PREPARATION TIME: 30 MINUTES   COOKING TIME: 10 MINUTES

NOTE: If you overcook the potatoes, drain them carefully and spread out on a large flat dish or tray and cool completely. Most of the potatoes will firm up if you do this. In this case, you should also take a little extra care when stirring in the mayonnaise.

CHICKPEA AND ROAST VEGETABLE SALAD

500 g (1 lb 2 oz) butternut pumpkin
(squash), cut into chunks
2 red capsicums (peppers), halved
4 eggplants (aubergines), halved lengthways
4 zucchini (courgettes), halved lengthways
4 onions, cut into quarters
olive oil, for brushing
600 g (1 lb 5 oz) tinned chickpeas, rinsed
and drained
2 tablespoons chopped flat-leaf
(Italian) parsley

DRESSING
80 ml (2³/4 fl oz/¹/3 cup) olive oil
2 tablespoons lemon juice
1 garlic clove, crushed
1 tablespoon chopped thyme

SERVES 8

Preheat the oven to 220°C (425°F/Gas 7). Brush two baking trays with oil and spread the vegetables in a single layer over the trays. Brush the vegetables lightly with the olive oil.

Bake for 40 minutes, or until the vegetables are tender and begin to brown slightly on the edges. Remove and set aside to cool. Remove the skins from the capsicum if you wish. Chop the capsicum, eggplant and zucchini into large pieces, then put all the vegetables in a bowl with the chickpeas and half the parsley.

Whisk together all the dressing ingredients in a bowl. Season, then toss through the vegetables. Set aside for 30 minutes to marinate. Spoon into a serving bowl and sprinkle with the rest of the parsley before serving.

PREPARATION TIME: 25 MINUTES   COOKING TIME: 40 MINUTES

HOT POTATO SALAD

4 bacon slices
1.5 kg (3 lb 5 oz) red potatoes, unpeeled
4 spring onions (scallions), sliced
3 tablespoons chopped flat-leaf
(Italian) parsley

DRESSING
170 ml (5¹/2 fl oz/²/3 cup) extra virgin olive oil
1 tablespoon dijon mustard
80 ml (2¹/2 fl oz/¹/3 cup) white wine
vinegar

SERVES 8

Trim the rind and any excess fat from the bacon, then cook under a hot grill (broiler) until crisp. Chop into small pieces.

Steam or boil the potatoes for 10-15 minutes, or until just tender. Don't let the skins break away. Drain and cool slightly.

To make the dressing, whisk all the ingredients together in a jug.

Cut the potatoes into quarters and place in a bowl with half the bacon, the spring onion, parsley and some salt and freshly ground black pepper. Pour in half the dressing and toss to coat the potatoes thoroughly. Transfer to a serving bowl, drizzle with the remaining dressing and sprinkle the remaining bacon over the top.

PREPARATION TIME: 15 MINUTES   COOKING TIME: 25 MINUTES

Chickpea and roast vegetable salad

CARAMELIZED ONION AND POTATO SALAD

2 tablespoons oil
6 red onions, thinly sliced
1 kg (2 lb 4 oz) kipfler, desiree or pontiac potatoes
4 bacon slices
35 g (1¼ oz/¾ cup) chopped chives

MAYONNAISE
250 g (9 oz/1 cup) whole-egg mayonnaise
1 tablespoon dijon mustard
2-3 tablespoons lemon juice
2 tablespoons sour cream

SERVES 10–12

Heat the oil in a large heavy-based frying pan, add the onion and cook over low–medium heat for 40 minutes, or until caramelized.

Cut the potatoes into large chunks (if small, leave them whole) and steam or boil for 5-10 minutes until just tender (pierce with the point of a small knife — if the potato comes away easily, it is ready). Drain and cool slightly.

Remove the rind from the bacon and grill (broil) until crisp. Drain on crumpled paper towels and cool slightly before roughly chopping.

Put the potato, onion and chives in a large bowl, reserving a few chives for garnish, and toss to combine.

To make the mayonnaise, whisk the ingredients together in a bowl. Pour over the salad and toss to coat. Sprinkle with the bacon and garnish with the reserved chives.

PREPARATION TIME: 20 MINUTES   COOKING TIME: 50 MINUTES

NOTE: Ideal boiling potatoes are waxy in texture with a high moisture content and low starch content. You can also use sebago, coliban, pink fir apple and jersey royals.

Caramelized onion and potato salad

RICE SALAD

300 g (10½ oz/1½ cups) long-grain rice
80 g (2¾ oz/½ cup) fresh or frozen peas
3 spring onions (scallions), sliced
1 green capsicum (pepper), finely diced
1 red capsicum (pepper), finely diced
310 g (11 oz) tinned corn kernels, drained, rinsed
15 g (½ oz/¼ cup) chopped mint

DRESSING
125 ml (4 fl oz/½ cup) extra virgin olive oil
2 tablespoons lemon juice
1 garlic clove, crushed
1 teaspoon sugar

SERVES 6–8

Bring a large saucepan of water to the boil and stir in the rice. Return to the boil and cook for 12–15 minutes, or until tender. Drain and cool.

Cook the peas in a small saucepan of boiling water for about 2 minutes. Rinse under cold water and drain well.

For the dressing, whisk together the oil, juice, garlic and sugar in a small jug, then season.

Combine the rice, peas, spring onion, capsicum, corn and mint in a large bowl. Add the dressing and mix well. Cover and refrigerate for 1 hour. Transfer to a serving dish.

PREPARATION TIME: 30 MINUTES +   COOKING TIME: 20 MINUTES

COLESLAW

½ green (savoy) cabbage
¼ red cabbage
3 carrots, coarsely grated
6 radishes, coarsely grated
1 red capsicum (pepper), chopped
4 spring onions (scallions), sliced
3 tablespoons chopped flat-leaf (Italian) parsley
250 g (9 oz/1 cup) mayonnaise

SERVES 10

Remove the hard cores from the cabbages and thinly shred the leaves with a sharp knife. Place in a large bowl and add the carrot, radish, red capsicum, spring onion and parsley.

Add the mayonnaise, season with salt and freshly ground black pepper and toss well.

PREPARATION TIME: 20 MINUTES   COOKING TIME: NIL

NOTE: The vegetables can be chopped and refrigerated for up to 3 hours before serving. Add the mayonnaise just before serving.

CAESAR SALAD

1 small baguette
2 tablespoons olive oil
2 garlic cloves, halved
4 bacon slices (trimmed of fat)
2 cos (romaine) lettuces
10 anchovy fillets, halved lengthways
100 g (3½ oz/1 cup) shaved parmesan cheese
parmesan cheese shavings, extra, to serve

DRESSING
1 egg yolk
2 garlic cloves, crushed
2 teaspoons dijon mustard
2 anchovy fillets
2 tablespoons white wine vinegar
1 tablespoon worcestershire sauce
185 ml (6 fl oz/¾ cup) olive oil

SERVES 6

Preheat the oven to 180°C (350°F/Gas 4). To make the croutons, cut the baguette into 15 thin slices and brush both sides of each slice with oil. Spread them on a baking tray and bake for 10–15 minutes, or until golden brown. Leave to cool slightly, then rub each side of each slice with the cut edge of a garlic clove. The baked bread can then be broken roughly into pieces or cut into small cubes.

Cook the bacon under a hot grill (broiler) until crisp. Drain on paper towels until cooled, then break into chunky pieces.

Tear the lettuce into pieces and put in a large serving bowl with the bacon, anchovies, croutons and parmesan.

To make the dressing, place the egg yolks, garlic, mustard, anchovies, vinegar and worcestershire sauce in a food processor or blender. Season and process for 20 seconds, or until smooth. With the motor running, add enough oil in a thin stream to make the dressing thick and creamy.

Drizzle the dressing over the salad and toss very gently until well distributed. Sprinkle the parmesan shavings over the top.

PREPARATION TIME: 25 MINUTES   COOKING TIME: 20 MINUTES

TOMATO AND BOCCONCINI SALAD

12 ripe roma (plum) tomatoes
10 bocconcini (fresh baby mozzarella cheese)
1 handful basil leaves

DRESSING
125 ml (4 fl oz/1/2 cup) extra virgin olive oil
80 ml (2 1/2 fl oz/1/3 cup) balsamic vinegar

SERVES 6–8

Cut the tomatoes lengthways into 3–4 slices (discard the outside slices, which won't lie flat). Slice each bocconcini lengthways into 3–4 slices. Arrange some tomato slices on a serving plate, place a bocconcini slice on top of each and scatter with some basil leaves. Repeat until all the tomato, bocconcini and basil have been used. Season with salt and pepper.

To make the dressing, whisk the oil and vinegar together. Drizzle over the salad.

PREPARATION TIME: 15 MINUTES   COOKING TIME: NIL

NOTE: This salad can also be served with a pesto dressing. Finely chop 1 large handful basil leaves, 2 tablespoons pine nuts, 50 g (1 3/4 oz/1/2 cup) grated parmesan cheese and 2 crushed garlic cloves in a food processor. With the motor running, add 125 ml (4 fl oz/1/2 cup) olive oil and 2 tablespoons lemon juice in a steady stream.

ASPARAGUS AND HAZELNUT SALAD

95 g (3 1/4 oz/2/3 cup) hazelnuts
300 g (10 1/2 oz) asparagus

DRESSING
60 ml (2 fl oz/1/4 cup) olive oil
3 teaspoons white wine vinegar

SERVES 4

Toast the hazelnuts in a frying pan over medium heat for 3 minutes, shaking the pan to prevent the nuts burning. Lightly crush the nuts in a mortar and pestle.

Cook the asparagus in a large saucepan of boiling water for 1 minute. Drain and plunge into iced water. Drain.

Mix the olive oil and white wine vinegar in a screw-top jar. Season and drizzle over the asparagus. Sprinkle with the nuts.

PREPARATION TIME: 10 MINUTES   COOKING TIME: 4 MINUTES

BEAN SALAD

s250 g (9 oz) green beans, trimmed
400 g (14 oz) tinned chickpeas
425 g (15 oz) tinned red kidney beans
400 g (14 oz) tinned cannellini beans
270 g (9½ oz) tinned corn kernels
3 spring onions (scallions), sliced
1 red capsicum (pepper), finely chopped
3 celery sticks, chopped
4-6 bottled gherkins (pickles), chopped
(optional)
3 tablespoons chopped mint
3 tablespoons chopped flat-leaf
(Italian) parsley

MUSTARD VINAIGRETTE
125 ml (4 fl oz/½ cup) extra virgin olive oil
2 tablespoons white wine vinegar
1 teaspoon sugar
1 tablespoon dijon mustard
1 garlic clove, crushed

SERVES 8–10

Cut the green beans into short lengths. Bring a small pan of water to the boil and cook the beans for 2 minutes. Drain and rinse, then leave in a bowl of iced water until cold. Drain well.

Drain and rinse the chickpeas, kidney beans, cannellini beans and corn kernels. Mix them in a large bowl with the green beans, spring onion, capsicum, celery, gherkin, mint and parsley. Season with salt and freshly ground black pepper.

To make the vinaigrette, whisk together the oil, white wine vinegar and sugar in a small jug. Season with salt and black pepper. Whisk in the mustard and garlic. Drizzle over the salad and toss gently.

PREPARATION TIME: 30 MINUTES   COOKING TIME: 2 MINUTES

WALDORF SALAD

2 green apples, cut into small pieces
2 red apples, cut into small pieces
2 tablespoons lemon juice
4 celery sticks, sliced
30 g (1 oz/¼ cup) walnut pieces
250 g (9 oz/1 cup) whole-egg mayonnaise
chopped flat-leaf (Italian) parsley,
to garnish (optional)

SERVES 4–6

Put the apple in a large bowl, drizzle with the lemon juice and toss to coat (this prevents the apples from discolouring). Mix in the celery and most of the walnut pieces.

Add the mayonnaise to the bowl and toss until well coated. Season to taste. Spoon the salad into a serving bowl, sprinkle with the remaining walnut pieces and serve. Garnish with parsley.

PREPARATION TIME: 20 MINUTES   COOKING TIME: NIL

PESTO PASTA SALAD

2 large handfuls basil leaves
2 garlic cloves, crushed
50 g (1¾ oz/½ cup) grated parmesan
cheese
2 tablespoons pine nuts, toasted
80 ml (2½ fl oz/⅓ cup) olive oil
500 g (1 lb 2 oz) penne, cooked
250 g (9 oz) cherry tomatoes, halved
1 small red onion, sliced into thin wedges
150 g (5½ oz) black olives
parmesan cheese shavings, to garnish

SERVES 6–8

Process the basil in a food processor with the garlic, parmesan and pine nuts until roughly chopped. With the motor running, gradually add the olive oil in a thin stream until well combined.

Place the pasta in a large bowl, stir in the pesto and mix well. Add the tomatoes, onion and olives and stir gently. Spoon into a serving dish and garnish with parmesan.

PREPARATION TIME: 25 MINUTES   COOKING TIME: 15 MINUTES

DESSERTS

CHOC-GINGER PUDDINGS

320 g (11¼ oz/2 cups) raisins, chopped
200 g (7 oz/1⅓ cups) currants
110 g (3¾ oz/⅔ cup) pitted dates, chopped
75 g (2½ oz/⅓ cup) glacé (candied) ginger, chopped
160 g (5¾ oz/1 cup) sultanas (golden raisins)
100 g (3½ oz) dried pears, chopped
100 g (3½ oz) dried apricots, chopped
175 g (6 oz/1 cup) dark chocolate bits
75 g (2½ oz/½ cup) pistachios, chopped
125 ml (4 fl oz/½ cup) brandy
250 g (9 oz) unsalted butter, frozen and grated
185 g (6½ oz/1 cup) dark brown sugar
1 tablespoon treacle or molasses
80 ml (2¾ fl oz/⅓ cup) orange juice
1 teaspoon finely grated orange zest
80 ml (2¾ fl oz/⅓ cup) lemon juice
1 teaspoon finely grated lemon zest
4 eggs, lightly beaten
1 teaspoon bicarbonate of soda (baking soda)
185 g (6½ oz/1½ cups) plain (all-purpose) flour
60 g (2¼ oz/½ cup) self-raising flour
2 teaspoons mixed (pumpkin pie) spice
2 teaspoons ground cinnamon
1 teaspoon freshly grated nutmeg
80 g (2¾ oz/1 cup) fresh breadcrumbs
pouring (whipping) cream, to serve (optional)

MAKES 10

Put all the fruit, chocolate and pistachios into a large basin and stir in the brandy. Cover with plastic wrap and leave overnight.

Bring 2 large saucepans of water to the boil. Cut a piece of calico into ten 30 cm (12 inch) squares. Put the calico in one of the saucepans of boiling water for 15 minutes, then remove with tongs and, with gloved hands, wring out the water.

Put the butter in a large bowl and stir in the sugar, treacle, zests and juices and the eggs. Add the combined sifted bicarbonate of soda, flours and spices in two batches. Stir in the fruit and breadcrumbs.

Place a calico square on a flat surface and rub liberally with plain flour, leaving a border of calico. Place a loosely packed cup of the mixture into the centre of the cloth. Gather and tie the cloth into a neat ball, pleating the calico. Tie firmly with string around the top and tie the end of the string to enable you to hang the puddings from a wooden spoon. Repeat with all the mixture and calico. Place half the puddings in each saucepan of boiling water, then sit the lids over the spoons to keep most of the steam in. Simmer for 1 hour. Hang overnight in a cool place to dry, then refrigerate in an airtight container. Keep for up to 1 month.

To reheat, lower the puddings into a pan of boiling water and boil for 30 minutes. Remove the cloths and serve individually, with cream.

PREPARATION TIME: 45 MINUTES +   COOKING TIME: 1 HOUR 15 MINUTES

SUMMER BERRIES IN CHAMPAGNE JELLY

1 litre (35 fl oz/4 cups) Champagne or sparkling white wine
1½ tablespoons powdered gelatine
250 g (9 oz/1 cup) sugar
4 strips lemon zest
4 strips orange zest
250 g (9 oz/1⅔ cups) small strawberries, hulled
250 g (9 oz/1⅔ cups) blueberries

SERVES 8

Pour half the Champagne into a bowl and let the bubbles subside. Sprinkle the gelatine over the top in an even layer. Leave until the gelatine is spongy — do not stir. Pour the remaining Champagne into a large saucepan, add the sugar and zests and heat gently, stirring constantly, until all the sugar has dissolved.

Remove the saucepan from the heat, add the gelatine mixture and stir until thoroughly dissolved. Leave to cool completely, then remove the zest.

Divide the berries among eight 125 ml (4 fl oz/½ cup) stemmed wine glasses and gently pour the jelly over them. Refrigerate until set. Remove from the refrigerator 15 minutes before serving.

PREPARATION TIME: 10 MINUTES +   COOKING TIME: 5 MINUTES

TIRAMISU

500 ml (17 fl oz/2 cups) strong black coffee, cooled
60 ml (2 fl oz/¼ cup) Marsala or coffee-flavoured liqueur
2 eggs, separated
60 g (2¼ oz/¼ cup) caster (superfine) sugar
250 g (9 oz) mascarpone cheese
250 ml (9 fl oz/1 cup) pouring (whipping) cream
16 large savoiardi (lady fingers) biscuits
2 tablespoons dark unsweetened cocoa powder

SERVES 6

Combine the coffee and Marsala in a bowl and set aside. Beat the egg yolks and sugar in a bowl with electric beaters for 3 minutes, or until thick and pale. Add the mascarpone and mix until just combined. Transfer to a large bowl. Beat the cream in a separate bowl, with electric beaters, until soft peaks form, then fold into the mascarpone mixture.

Place the egg whites in a clean, dry bowl and beat with electric beaters until soft peaks form. Fold quickly and lightly into the cream mixture.

Dip half the biscuits into the coffee mixture, drain off any excess and arrange in the base of a 2.5 litre (84 fl oz/10 cup) ceramic or glass serving dish. Spread half the cream mixture over the biscuits.

Dip the remaining biscuits into the remaining coffee mixture and repeat the layers. Smooth the surface and dust liberally with the cocoa powder. Refrigerate overnight.

PREPARATION TIME: 30 MINUTES +   COOKING TIME: NIL

Summer berries in Champagne jelly

ICE CREAM BOMBE

1 large mango, finely chopped
160 g (5½ oz/1 cup) tinned pineapple pieces, drained
60 ml (2 fl oz/¼ cup) Grand Marnier
250 g (9 oz) fresh strawberries, puréed
400 g (14 oz) tin condensed milk
600 ml (21 fl oz) pouring (whipping) cream
80 g (2¾ oz) dessert nougat, chopped
35 g (1¼ oz/¼ cup) roughly chopped unsalted pistachios
strawberries, extra, halved, to garnish

TOFFEE BARK
90 g (3¼ oz/⅓ cup) caster (superfine) sugar

SERVES 8

Lightly grease a 2 litre (70 fl oz/8 cup) pudding basin steamed pudding mould) and line with plastic wrap, allowing it to hang over the side of the basin. Put in the freezer until ready to use. Drain the mango and pineapple in a sieve.

Mix the Grand Marnier, strawberry purée and condensed milk in a large bowl. Whisk the cream to soft peaks, then add to the bowl and continue whisking until thick. Fold in the drained fruits, nougat and pistachios. Pour the mixture into the pudding basin, cover with plastic wrap and freeze overnight, or until firm.

To serve, remove the plastic wrap from the base and invert the pudding onto a chilled serving plate. Remove the bowl, but leave the plastic wrap and refrigerate for 15–25 minutes to soften slightly.

For the toffee bark, line a baking tray with baking paper. Heat the sugar over low heat in a heavy-based saucepan for 2–3 minutes, or until melted and golden. Carefully pour onto the tray. Tilt the tray to get a thin, even layer of toffee over the paper and cool slightly. While still pliable, drape the paper over a rolling pin and allow to cool for 30–60 seconds before peeling away strips of toffee in large irregular shapes. Cool. To serve, remove the plastic and decorate the bombe with toffee bark and strawberries.

PREPARATION TIME: 20 MINUTES +   COOKING TIME: 3 MINUTES

NOTE: Dessert nougat is a soft nougat available at confectionery shops and some delicatessens.

ROCKY ROAD

250 g (9 oz) pink and white
marshmallows, halved
160 g (5³/4 oz/1 cup) unsalted peanuts,
roughly chopped
105 g (3¹/2 oz/¹/2 cup) glacé (candied)
cherries, halved
60 g (2¹/4 oz/1 cup) shredded coconut
350 g (12 oz) dark chocolate, chopped

MAKES ABOUT 30 PIECES

Line the base and two opposite sides of a shallow 20 cm (8 inch) square cake tin with foil.

Put all the marshmallows, peanuts, cherries and coconut into a large bowl and mix until well combined.

Put the chocolate in a heatproof bowl. Half-fill a saucepan with water and bring to the boil. Remove from the heat and place the bowl over the pan, making sure it is not touching the water. Stir occasionally until the chocolate is melted.

Add the chocolate to the marshmallow mixture and toss until well combined. Spoon into the cake tin and press evenly over the base. Refrigerate for several hours, or until set. Carefully lift out of the tin, then peel away the foil and cut the rocky road into small pieces. Store in an airtight container in the refrigerator.

PREPARATION TIME: 20 MINUTES + COOKING TIME: 5 MINUTES

OLIEBOLLEN

7 g (¹/4 oz) sachet dry yeast
1 tablespoon caster (superfine) sugar
250 ml (9 fl oz/1 cup) milk, warmed
280 g (10 oz/2¹/4 cups) plain
(all-purpose) flour
120 g (4 oz/³/4 cup) raisins, chopped
1 green apple, peeled and diced
45 g (1¹/2 oz/¹/4 cup) mixed peel (mixed
candied citrus peel)
2 eggs, lightly beaten
2 teaspoons finely grated lemon zest
oil, for deep-frying
caster (superfine) sugar, for coating

MAKES ABOUT 48

Place the yeast, 1 teaspoon of the sugar and 60 ml (2 fl oz/¹/4 cup) of the milk in a bowl and stir. Leave in a warm place for about 10 minutes, until frothy. Sift the flour into a large bowl and stir in the remaining sugar, raisins, apple and peel. Make a well in the centre and pour in the remaining milk, the yeast mixture, eggs and lemon zest. Mix with a flat-bladed knife to a soft sticky batter. Cover and leave to prove for 30 minutes. Stir the mixture thoroughly before cooking.

Fill a deep heavy-based saucepan one-third full of oil and heat to moderate 180°C (350°F), or until a cube of bread dropped into the oil browns in 15 seconds. Drop walnut-sized balls of dough from a tablespoon into the hot oil. Cook in several batches until well browned and cooked through. Drain well on crumpled paper towels, then toss lightly in caster sugar. Serve while still warm.

PREPARATION TIME: 20 MINUTES + COOKING TIME: 15 MINUTES

STEAMED PUDDING

640 g (1 lb 7 oz/4 cups) mixed sultanas (golden raisins), currants and raisins
330 g (11½ oz/1⅔ cups) mixed dried fruit, chopped
45 g (1½ oz/¼ cup) mixed peel (mixed candied citrus peel)
125 ml (4 fl oz/½ cup) brown ale
2 tablespoons rum or brandy
80 ml (2½ fl oz/⅓ cup) orange juice
80 ml (2½ fl oz/⅓ cup) lemon juice
1 teaspoon finely grated orange zest
1 teaspoon finely grated lemon zest
225 g (8 oz) suet, grated
245 g (8½ oz/1⅓ cups) soft brown sugar
3 eggs, lightly beaten
200 g (7 oz/2½ cups) fresh white breadcrumbs
90 g (3¼ oz/¾ cup) self-raising flour
1 teaspoon mixed (pumpkin pie) spice
¼ teaspoon grated nutmeg
100 g (3½ oz/⅔ cup) blanched almonds, roughly chopped

SERVES 10–12

Put the sultanas, currants, raisins, mixed dried fruit, mixed peel, brown ale, rum, orange and lemon juices and zests into a large bowl and stir together. Cover and leave overnight.

Add the suet, brown sugar, eggs, breadcrumbs, flour, spices, almonds and a pinch of salt to the bowl and mix well. The mixture should fall from the spoon — if it is too stiff, add a little more ale.

Put a 2 litre (70 fl oz/8 cups) pudding basin (steamed pudding mould) on a trivet or upturned saucer in a large saucepan with a lid, and pour in enough water to come halfway up the side of the basin. Remove the basin and put the water on to boil.

Fill the pudding basin with the pudding mixture. To cover the pudding, place a sheet of foil on the bench, top with a piece of baking paper and brush the paper with melted butter. Fold a pleat across the centre of the foil and paper. Put the paper and foil, foil side up, over the basin. Tie a double length of string firmly around the rim of the basin, then tie a double length of string onto that string to form a handle to lower the pudding into the water. If you have a basin with a lid, clip it on at this stage. The paper/foil lid prevents any moisture from getting into the pudding and making it soggy.

Using the handle, carefully lower the pudding into the saucepan and reduce the heat until the water is simmering quickly. Cover the saucepan. Steam the pudding for 8 hours, replenishing with boiling water when necessary. If you want to keep your pudding and reheat it later, then steam it for 6 hours and steam it for another 2 hours on the day you would like to eat it. Store in a cool, dry place for up to 3 months.

PREPARATION TIME: 40 MINUTES +   COOKING TIME: 8 HOURS

NOTE: Buy suet from your butcher.

FRESH FRUIT PAVLOVA

6 egg whites
500 g (1 lb 2 oz/2¹/₃ cups) caster (superfine) sugar
1¹/₂ tablespoons cornflour (cornstarch)
1¹/₂ teaspoons vinegar
500 ml (17 fl oz/2 cups) pouring (whipping) cream, whipped
2 bananas, sliced
500 g (1 lb 2 oz) strawberries, sliced
4 kiwi fruit, sliced
4 passionfruit, pulp removed

SERVES 6–8

Preheat the oven to 150°C (300°F/Gas 2). Line a large baking tray with baking paper and draw a 26 cm (10¹/₂ inch) circle on the paper. Turn the paper over and place on the tray. Beat the egg whites with electric beaters in a large dry bowl until soft peaks form. Gradually add all but 2 tablespoons of the sugar, beating well after each addition. Combine the cornflour and vinegar with the last of the sugar and beat for 1 minute before adding it to the bowl. Beat for 5–10 minutes, or until all the sugar has dissolved and the meringue is stiff and glossy. Spread onto the paper inside the circle. Shape the meringue evenly, running the flat side of a palette knife along the edge and over the top.

Bake for 40 minutes, or until pale and crisp. Reduce the heat to 120°C (250°F/Gas ¹/₂) and bake for 15 minutes. Turn off the oven and cool the pavlova in the oven, keeping the door slightly ajar. When cooled, top with cream and fruit. Drizzle with passionfruit pulp and serve.

PREPARATION TIME: 30 MINUTES   COOKING TIME: 55 MINUTES

CRANBERRY KISEL

2 lemons
375 g (13 oz/1¹/₂ cups) caster (superfine) sugar
2 cinnamon sticks
600 g (1 lb 5 oz) cranberries (fresh or frozen)
2 teaspoons cornflour (cornstarch)
2 teaspoons orange juice

YOGHURT CREAM
250 ml (9 fl oz/1 cup) pouring (whipping) cream
125 ml (4 fl oz/¹/₂ cup) plain yoghurt
115 g (4 oz/¹/₂ cup) soft brown sugar

SERVES 4

Remove the peel from the lemons in strips with a vegetable peeler. Put the peel, sugar, cinnamon sticks and 375 ml (13 fl oz/1¹/₂ cups) water into a saucepan over low heat and stir. Bring to the boil, then simmer for 5 minutes.

Add the cranberries to the hot syrup, return to the boil and simmer for 10 minutes, or until the skins have split. Remove from the heat and set aside to cool. Remove and discard the peel and cinnamon sticks. Remove about 80 g (2³/₄ oz/¹/₂ cup) of the berries and reserve. Blend or process the remaining mixture until smooth, return to the saucepan and add the reserved whole berries. Blend the cornflour and orange juice in a bowl, add to the purée, then stir over medium heat for 5 minutes, or until the mixture boils and thickens. Serve with yoghurt cream.

To make the yoghurt cream, beat the cream in a bowl until soft peaks form, then fold the yoghurt through. Transfer to a small bowl and sprinkle with the sugar. Refrigerate, covered, for 2 hours.

PREPARATION TIME: 15 MINUTES +   COOKING TIME: 15 MINUTES

CHOCOLATE HAZELNUT TORTE

500 g (1 lb 2 oz) dark chocolate, chopped
6 eggs
2 tablespoons Frangelico
165 g (5½ oz/1½ cups) ground hazelnuts
250 ml (9 fl oz/1 cup) pouring (whipping) cream, whipped
12 whole hazelnuts, lightly roasted

CHOCOLATE TOPPING
200 g (7 oz) dark chocolate, chopped
185 ml (6 fl oz/¾ cup) pouring (whipping) cream
1 tablespoon Frangelico

SERVES 10

Preheat the oven to 150°C (300°F/Gas 2). Grease a deep 20 cm (8 inch) round cake tin and line with baking paper.

Put the chocolate in a heatproof bowl. Half-fill a saucepan with water and bring to the boil. Remove from the heat and place the bowl over the pan, making sure it is not touching the water. Stir occasionally until the chocolate is melted. Put the eggs in a large heatproof bowl and add the Frangelico. Place the bowl over a saucepan of barely simmering water over low heat, making sure it does not touch the water. Beat with an electric mixer on high speed for 7 minutes, or until the mixture is light and foamy. Remove from the heat. Using a metal spoon, quickly and lightly fold the melted chocolate and ground nuts into the egg mixture until just combined. Fold in the cream and pour the mixture into the tin. Place the tin in a shallow baking dish. Pour in enough hot water to come halfway up the side of the tin.

Bake for 1 hour, or until just set. Remove the tin from the baking dish. Cool to room temperature, cover with plastic wrap and refrigerate overnight.

Cut a 17 cm (7 inch) circle from heavy cardboard. Invert the chilled cake onto the disc so that the base of the cake becomes the top. Place on a wire rack over a baking tray and remove the baking paper. Allow the cake to return to room temperature before you start to decorate.

To make the topping, combine the chopped chocolate, cream and Frangelico in a small pan. Heat gently over low heat, stirring, until the chocolate is melted and the mixture is smooth. Pour the chocolate mixture over the cake in the centre, tilting slightly to cover the cake evenly. Tap the baking tray gently on the bench so that the top is level and the icing runs completely down the side of the cake. Place the hazelnuts around the edge of the cake. Refrigerate just until the topping has set and the cake is firm. Carefully transfer the cake to a serving plate, and cut into thin wedges to serve.

PREPARATION TIME: 1 HOUR +   COOKING TIME: 1 HOUR 15 MINUTES

ICE CREAM PUDDING

50 g (1³/4 oz/¹/3 cup) toasted almonds, chopped
45 g (1¹/2 oz/¹/4 cup) mixed peel (mixed candied citrus peel)
80 g (2³/4 oz/¹/2 cup) raisins, chopped
80 g (2³/4 oz/¹/2 cup) sultanas (golden raisins)
50 g (1³/4 oz/¹/3 cup) currants
80 ml (2¹/2 fl oz/¹/3 cup) rum
1 litre (35 fl oz/4 cups) good-quality vanilla ice cream
105 g (3¹/2 oz/¹/2 cup) red and green glacé (candied) cherries, quartered
1 teaspoon mixed (pumpkin pie) spice
1 teaspoon ground cinnamon
¹/2 teaspoon freshly grated nutmeg
1 litre (35 fl oz/4 cups) chocolate ice cream

SERVES 10

Mix the almonds, peel, raisins, sultanas, currants and rum in a bowl, cover with plastic wrap and leave overnight. Chill a 2 litre (70 fl oz/8 cups) pudding basin (steamed pudding mould) in the freezer overnight.

Soften the vanilla ice cream slightly and mix in the glacé cherries. Working quickly, press the ice cream around the inside of the chilled basin, spreading it evenly to cover the base and side of the basin. Return the basin to the freezer and leave overnight. Check the ice cream a couple of times and spread it evenly to the top.

The next day, mix the spices and chocolate ice cream with the fruit mixture. Spoon it into the centre of the pudding bowl and smooth the top. Freeze overnight, or until very firm. Turn out the pudding onto a chilled plate and decorate. Cut into wedges, to serve.

PREPARATION TIME: 1 HOUR +   COOKING TIME: NIL

SHERRY TRIFLE

85 g (3 oz) packet strawberry jelly crystals (gelatin dessert)
300 g (10¹/2 oz) jam Swiss roll (jelly roll)
80 ml (2¹/2 fl oz/¹/3 cup) sherry
825 g (1 lb 13 oz) tinned sliced peaches, drained
30 g (1 oz/¹/4 cup) instant custard powder
250 ml (9 fl oz/1 cup) milk
60 g (2¹/4 oz/¹/4 cup) caster (superfine) sugar
2 teaspoons vanilla essence
250 ml (9 fl oz/1 cup) pouring (whipping) cream
powdered drinking chocolate, to garnish
strawberries, optional, to garnish

SERVES 8

Make the jelly according to the packet directions and refrigerate until the mixture reaches the consistency of egg white. Cut the sponge roll into 1 cm (¹/2 inch) slices and arrange around the side and base of a 2.5 litre (84 fl oz/10 cup) glass bowl. Drizzle sherry over the sponge pieces.

Pour the jelly over the cake and refrigerate until set. When set, top with the peach slices and refrigerate. Blend the custard powder with 125 ml (4 fl oz/¹/2 cup) of the milk in a saucepan until smooth. Add the remaining milk, sugar and vanilla. Stir over medium heat for 5 minutes, or until the mixture thickens, then pour into a bowl and cool, stirring often. When cold, pour and spread the custard over the peaches. Refrigerate until cold.

Beat the cream in a bowl with electric beaters until soft peaks form, spread over the custard, forming peaks, then sprinkle with drinking chocolate. Decorate with strawberries, if desired.

PREPARATION TIME: 30 MINUTES +   COOKING TIME: 10 MINUTES

KOEKSISTERS

SYRUP
875 g (1 lb 15 oz/3½ cups) caster
(superfine) sugar
1 cinnamon stick
2 teaspoons lemon juice

435 g (15½ oz/3½ cups) self-raising flour
1 teaspoon ground cinnamon
1 tablespoon caster (superfine) sugar
50 g (1¾ oz) butter, chopped
2 eggs, lightly beaten
250 ml (9 fl oz/1 cup) milk
oil, for deep-frying

MAKES ABOUT 12

Combine the sugar, cinnamon stick, lemon juice and 375 ml (13 fl oz/
1½ cups) water in a saucepan and stir over medium heat until the sugar
has dissolved. Bring to the boil, then reduce the heat and simmer for
5–7 minutes, or until thick and syrupy. Remove and leave until cold.

Sift the flour and cinnamon into a large bowl, stir in the sugar and add the
butter. Rub the butter into the flour with your fingertips until the mixture
resembles fine breadcrumbs. Make a well in the centre, add the eggs
and milk and mix with a flat-bladed knife, using a cutting action, until
the mixture comes together in clumps. Gather together and knead on
a lightly floured surface for 1 minute, or until smooth. Place in a large
lightly oiled bowl, cover and leave for 1 hour.

Roll the dough out into a 30 x 40 cm (12 x 16 inch) rectangle. Cut the
dough in half crossways, then cut each half into quarters. Cut each
quarter into nine 10 cm (4 inch) long strips. Plait three strips together,
pinching the ends firmly to seal. Repeat with the remaining strips.

Fill a deep heavy-based saucepan one-third full of oil and heat to
170°C (325°F), or until a cube of bread dropped into the oil browns in
20 seconds. Fry the plaits in several batches for about 2–3 minutes, or
until well browned and cooked though. Drain on crumpled paper towels.
While still hot, dip each into the cold syrup for about 5 seconds, turning
to coat evenly. Drain on a wire cake rack over a baking tray. Although
best eaten on the day they are made, they can be eaten the next day,
heated and brushed with any remaining syrup.

PREPARATION TIME: 20 MINUTES +   COOKING TIME: 15 MINUTES

BOILED PUDDING

310 g (11 oz/1²/₃ cups) mixed dried fruit

45 g (1½ oz/¼ cup) mixed peel (mixed candied citrus peel)

640 g (1 lb 7 oz/4 cups) mixed sultanas (golden raisins), currants and raisins

125 ml (4 fl oz/½ cup) brown ale

2 tablespoons rum or brandy

2 tablespoons orange juice

2 tablespoons lemon juice

1 tablespoon grated orange zest

1 tablespoon grated lemon zest

225 g (8 oz) suet, grated

245 g (9 oz/1⅓ cups) soft brown sugar

3 eggs, lightly beaten

200 g (7 oz/2½ cups) white breadcrumbs

90 g (3¼ oz/¾ cup) self-raising flour

1 teaspoon mixed (pumpkin pie) spice

¼ teaspoon freshly grated nutmeg

100 g (3½ oz/²/₃ cup) blanched almonds, chopped

Finely chop the mixed dried fruit and put in a bowl with the mixed peel, sultanas, currants, raisins, ale, rum, orange and lemon juice and zest. Cover and leave overnight. Mix the fruit with the remaining ingredients and a pinch of salt. Leave for 10 minutes.

Cut an 80 cm (32 inch) square from a piece of calico. Add the calico to the saucepan and simmer for 20 minutes. Remove the calico from the boiling water and wring out well. Spread out the calico on a work surface. Cover with flour. Spoon the fruit mixture into the centre of the cloth. Bring the points of the cloth together over the top and gather in the material. Leaving room at the top for expansion, tie the top with string. Tie another length of string around the top, long enough to tie to the handles on either side of the pan to suspend the pudding. Lower the pudding into the simmering water. Cover, place a few tins of fruit on the lid, and boil the pudding for 5 hours. Replenish with boiling water when necessary. Remove from the water and hang. Hook up the calico ends. Leave the pudding hanging overnight to dry. Untie the cloth and spread it out to make sure it dries. When it is dry, re-wrap and tie with string. The pudding will store, hanging in a cool, dry place for up to 4 months. To serve, boil for 2 hours, hang for 15 minutes, then remove from the cloth.

SERVES 10–12   PREPARATION TIME: 40 MINUTES +   COOKING TIME: 5 HOURS

CREAMED RICE WITH HOT CHERRY SAUCE

220 g (7³/₄ oz/1 cup) short-grain rice

1 litre (35 fl oz/4 cups) milk

1 tablespoon vanilla sugar

2 tablespoons caster (superfine) sugar

315 ml (11 fl oz/1¼ cups) pouring (whipping) cream

2 tablespoons whole blanched almonds

DARK CHERRY SAUCE

3 teaspoons cornflour (cornstarch)

425 g (15 oz) tinned stoneless black cherries in syrup

Put the rice and milk in a saucepan, cover and cook over low heat for 40-45 minutes, or until the rice is cooked. Remove from the heat and stir in both the sugars. Spoon into a bowl, cover the top of the rice with plastic wrap and cool. Beat the cream in a bowl with electric beaters until soft peaks form. Fold into the creamed rice. Reserve one whole almond and roughly chop the rest. Fold into the rice and stir in the whole almond. Refrigerate the rice while preparing the sauce.

To make the sauce, blend the cornflour with 2 tablespoons water in a bowl. Pour the cherries and their juice into a saucepan, add the cornflour mixture and stir over medium heat until the mixture boils. Remove from the heat. Spoon the rice into bowls and top with the sauce.

SERVES 6   PREPARATION TIME: 15 MINUTES +   COOKING TIME: 50 MINUTES

KLEJNE

500 g (1 lb 2 oz/4 cups) plain
(all-purpose) flour
1¼ teaspoons baking powder
¼ teaspoon bicarbonate of soda
(baking soda)
½ teaspoon ground cinnamon
125 g (4½ oz/½ cup) caster
(superfine) sugar
1 teaspoon finely grated lemon zest
100 g (3½ oz) butter, melted
250 ml (9 fl oz/1 cup) milk
oil, for deep-frying
icing (confectioners') sugar, for dusting

MAKES ABOUT 50

Sift the flour, baking powder, bicarbonate of soda and cinnamon into a bowl and stir in the sugar and lemon zest. Make a well in the centre and stir in the butter. Add enough milk to make a soft dough. Turn out onto a lightly floured surface and press together until the dough comes together. Pat into a ball, wrap in plastic wrap and refrigerate for 1 hour.

Roll the dough on a lightly floured surface into a rectangular shape about 5 mm (¼ inch) thick. Trim the edges. Cut into strips at 3 cm (1¼ inch) intervals, then cut each strip on the diagonal into 8 cm (3 inch) lengths. Cut a slit in each strip, leaving 1 cm (½ inch) at each end. Poke one end through the slit and pull out the other side to form a twist in the pastry. Repeat with the remaining dough. Place the shapes on a tray covered with baking paper and refrigerate for 30 minutes, or until firm.

Fill a deep heavy-based saucepan one-third full of oil and heat to 180°C (350°F), or until a cube of bread dropped into the oil browns in 15 seconds. Fry the biscuits in batches until well browned and cooked through. Drain on crumpled paper towels. Place on a tray covered with baking paper, cool to warm and dust lightly with icing sugar. Best eaten warm but can be eaten cold.

PREPARATION TIME: 25 MINUTES +   COOKING TIME: 15 MINUTES

NOTE: Originally German, these are now a favourite at Danish Christmas celebrations.

SUMMER PUDDING

150 g (5½ oz) blackcurrants
150 g (5½ oz) redcurrants
150 g (5½ oz) raspberries
150 g (5½ oz) blackberries
200 g (7 oz) strawberries, hulled and
quartered or halved
125 g (4½ oz/½ cup) caster (superfine)
sugar, or to taste
6-8 slices good-quality sliced white
bread, crusts removed

SERVES 6

Put all the berries, except the strawberries, in a saucepan with 125 ml (4 fl oz/½ cup) water and heat for 5 minutes, or until the berries begin to collapse. Add the strawberries and remove from the heat. Add the sugar, to taste. Allow to cool.

Line a 1 litre (35 fl oz/4 cup) pudding basin (steamed pudding mould) or six 170 ml (5½ oz/⅔ cup) moulds with the bread. For the large mould, cut a large circle out of one slice for the base and cut the rest of the bread into wide fingers. For the small moulds, use one slice of bread for each, cutting a small circle to fit the base and strips to fit snugly around the sides. Drain from a little of the juice off the fruit mixture. Dip one side of each piece of bread in the juice before fitting it, juice side down, into the basin, leaving no gaps. Do not squeeze or flatten the bread or it will not absorb the juices. Fill the centre of the basin with the fruit and add a little juice. Cover the top with the remaining dipped bread, juice side up, trimmed to fit. Cover with plastic wrap. Place a small plate, which fits inside the dish, onto the plastic wrap, then weigh it down with heavy tins or a glass bowl. Place on a baking tray to catch any juices. For the small moulds, cover with plastic and sit a small tin, or a similar weight, on top of each. Refrigerate overnight. Turn out the pudding/s and serve with any leftover fruit mixture.

PREPARATION TIME: 30 MINUTES +   COOKING TIME: 5 MINUTES

MANGO SORBET

250 g (9 oz/1 cup) caster
(superfine) sugar
2 tablespoons lemon juice
500 ml (17 fl oz/2 cups) mango purée,
or 3 medium mangoes, puréed

SERVES 4–6

Combine the sugar and 315 ml (10 fl oz/1¼ cups) water in a saucepan and stir over low heat to dissolve the sugar. Bring to the boil and boil for 2 minutes without stirring. Set aside to cool to room temperature. Add the lemon juice to the mango purée and slowly pour on the sugar syrup. Mix well. Pour into a shallow metal tray, cover with plastic wrap and freeze for 4-6 hours, or until firm.

Break up the mixture with a fork and process in a food processor until smooth. Spoon into an airtight container and freeze for 4-6 hours.

PREPARATION TIME: 20 MINUTES +   COOKING TIME: 4 MINUTES

NESSELRODE

5 egg yolks
185 g (6½ oz/¾ cup) caster
(superfine) sugar
1 litre (35 fl oz/4 cups) pouring (whipping)
cream
1 teaspoon vanilla essence
1 tablespoon brandy
165 g (5¾ oz/½ cup) chestnut purée
75 g (2½ oz/½ cup) currants
80 g (2¾ oz/½ cup) sultanas (golden
raisins)
60 g (2¼ oz/¼ cup) glacé (candied)
cherries, chopped
95 g (3¼ oz/½ cup) mixed peel (mixed
candied citrus peel)

TO DECORATE
toasted flaked almonds
selection of glacé (candied) cherries
(cut in halves), angelica, crystallized
violets or sugared
grapes, fresh fruit or sugared rose petals
250 ml (9 fl oz/1 cup) pouring (whipping)
cream, extra, whipped (optional)

SERVES 8

Beat the egg yolks and sugar together in a small bowl with electric beaters until pale, thick and fluffy. Pour half the cream into a saucepan and heat until almost boiling. Gradually pour onto the eggs and sugar, mixing well. Strain the mixture back into the clean pan and place over low heat.

Using a wooden spoon, stir constantly around the base and sides of the pan until the custard thickens slightly and coats the back of the spoon. Do not boil or the custard will curdle. Remove from the heat and stir in the vanilla and brandy. Add the chestnut purée and beat well to combine. Strain the mixture and allow to cool.

Beat the remaining cream in a bowl until soft peaks form and fold into the custard mixture.

Put the currants and sultanas in a bowl and cover completely with warm water.

Pour the cream mixture into a shallow metal tray and freeze for 2–3 hours, or until the mixture is just starting to freeze. Transfer to a large bowl or food processor, beat until smooth, then pour back into the tray and return to the freezer. Repeat this step three times. Before the final freezing, add the glacé cherries, mixed peel and the well-drained currants and sultanas, then mix thoroughly.

Lightly oil a 2 litre (70 fl oz/8 cup) charlotte mould, line with plastic, then pour in the cream mixture. Cover the surface with a piece of plastic and freeze for at least 8 hours, or until firm.

Invert the pudding onto a serving plate and carefully peel away the plastic. Decorate the sides with evenly spaced lines of toasted almonds, pieces of angelica, halved glacé cherries, crystallized violets or sugared fruits. The nesselrode can be put back in the freezer after it is decorated. When ready to serve, pile whipped cream over the top, then top that with piped whipped cream.

PREPARATION TIME: 25 MINUTES +   COOKING TIME: NIL

BERRY TRIFLE

550 g (1 lb 4 oz/1½ cups) redcurrant jelly
(gelatin dessert)
170 ml (5½ fl oz/⅔ cup) fresh
orange juice
600 ml (21 fl oz/2½ cups) pouring
(whipping) cream
250 g (9 oz) mascarpone cheese
30 g (1 oz/¼ cup) icing
(confectioners') sugar
1 teaspoon vanilla essence
¼ teaspoon ground cinnamon
250 g (9 oz) savoiardi (lady fingers)
biscuits
375 ml (13 fl oz/1½ cups) Marsala
400 g (14 oz) fresh raspberries
250 g (9 oz) large fresh strawberries,
hulled and quartered
400 g (14 oz) fresh blueberries

SERVES 8–10

Melt the redcurrant jelly in a small saucepan over medium heat. Remove from the heat, stir in the orange juice and set aside until the mixture reaches room temperature.

Put the cream, mascarpone, icing sugar, vanilla essence and cinnamon in a bowl and beat with electric beaters until soft peaks form.

Cut each biscuit in half crossways and dip each piece in the Marsala. Arrange half over the base of a 3.25 litre (110 fl oz/13 cups) serving bowl. Sprinkle a third of the combined berries over the biscuits and drizzle with half the remaining Marsala and a third of the redcurrant sauce. Spoon half the cream mixture over the sauce. Repeat the layering with the remaining half of the dipped biscuits and Marsala, a third of the berries and sauce, and the remaining cream.

Arrange the remaining berries over the cream in a mound in the centre of the bowl. Reserve the final third of the redcurrant sauce, cover and refrigerate. Cover the trifle with plastic wrap and refrigerate overnight. Before serving, pour the reserved redcurrant sauce over the berries to glaze. (Gently reheat the sauce if it is too thick.)

PREPARATION TIME: 35 MINUTES +   COOKING TIME: 5 MINUTES

BAKED CUSTARD

3 eggs
95 g (3¼ oz/½ cup) soft brown sugar
375 ml (13 fl oz/1½ cups) milk
125 ml (4 fl oz/½ cup) pouring (whipping)
cream
1 teaspoon vanilla essence
freshly grated nutmeg, to dust

SERVES 4

Preheat the oven to 180°C (350°F/Gas 4). Brush a 1 litre (35 fl oz/4 cup) ovenproof dish with melted butter. Whisk the eggs, sugar, milk, cream and vanilla essence in a bowl for 1 minute. Pour into the dish and place the dish in a shallow baking dish. Pour enough boiling water into the baking dish to come halfway up the side of the ovenproof dish. Place on the oven shelf, sprinkle the top of the custard with nutmeg and bake for 15 minutes. Reduce the heat to warm 160°C (315°F/Gas 2–3) and bake for a further 20 minutes, or until the custard is set. It should no longer be liquid but should wobble slightly when the dish is shaken lightly. Remove the dish from the water bath immediately. Serve warm or cold.

PREPARATION TIME: 5 MINUTES +   COOKING TIME: 35 MINUTES

PROFITEROLES WITH DARK CHOCOLATE SAUCE

60 g (2¼ oz) butter, chopped
90 g (3¼ oz/¾ cup) plain
(all-purpose) flour
3 eggs, lightly beaten

WHITE CHOCOLATE FILLING
30 g (1 oz/¼ cup) custard powder or
instant vanilla pudding mix
1 tablespoon caster (superfine) sugar
375 ml (13 fl oz/1½ cups) milk
150 g (5½ oz) white chocolate melts
(buttons), chopped
1 tablespoon Grand Marnier

DARK CHOCOLATE SAUCE
125 g (4½ oz) dark chocolate, chopped
125 ml (4 fl oz/½ cup) pouring (whipping)
cream

SERVES 4-6

Preheat the oven to 210°C (415°F/Gas 6-7). Line a baking tray with baking paper. Put the butter and 185 ml (6 fl oz/¾ cup) water in a saucepan. Bring to the boil, then remove from the heat. Add the flour all at once. Return to the heat and stir until the mixture forms a smooth ball. Set aside to cool slightly. Transfer to a bowl and, while beating with electric beaters, gradually add the eggs a little at a time, beating well after each addition, to form a thick, smooth, glossy paste.

Spoon 2 heaped teaspoons of the mixture onto the tray at 5 cm (2 inch) intervals. Sprinkle lightly with water and bake for 12-15 minutes, or until the dough is puffed. Turn off the oven. Pierce a small hole in the base of each profiterole with the point of a knife and return the profiteroles to the oven. Leave them to dry in the oven for 5 minutes.

To make the filling, combine the custard powder and sugar in a saucepan. Gradually add the milk, stirring until smooth, then continue to stir over low heat until the mixture boils and thickens. Remove from the heat and add the white chocolate and Grand Marnier. Stir until the chocolate is melted. Cover the surface with plastic wrap and allow to cool. Stir the custard until smooth, then spoon into a piping bag fitted with a 1 cm (½ inch) plain nozzle. Pipe the filling into each profiterole. Serve with the warm dark chocolate sauce.

For the dark chocolate sauce, combine the chocolate and cream in a small saucepan. Stir over low heat until the chocolate is melted and the mixture is smooth. Serve warm.

PREPARATION TIME: 40 MINUTES + COOLING   COOKING TIME: 50 MINUTES

NOTE: The profiteroles can be made a day ahead. Fill just before serving. You can also make miniature profiteroles, using 1 teaspoon of the mixture. Dip the tops of the cooked profiteroles in melted chocolate. When set, fill them with whipped cream.

FIG PUDDING

500 g (1 lb 2 oz) dried figs, chopped
440 ml (15$\frac{1}{4}$ fl oz/1$\frac{3}{4}$ cups) milk
240 g (8$\frac{1}{2}$ oz/3 cups) coarse fresh breadcrumbs
140 g (5 oz/$\frac{3}{4}$ cup) soft brown sugar
250 g (9 oz/2 cups) self-raising flour, sifted
2 eggs, lightly beaten
150 g (5$\frac{1}{2}$ oz) unsalted butter, melted and cooled

SERVES 8

Lightly grease a 2 litre (70 fl oz/8 cup) pudding basin (steamed pudding mould) with butter and line the base with baking paper. Place the empty basin in a saucepan on a trivet or upturned saucer and pour in enough water to come halfway up the side of the basin. Remove the basin and put the water on to boil.

Put the figs in a saucepan with the milk. Bring to a simmer, cover and cook over low heat for 10 minutes. Stir to combine. Combine the breadcrumbs, sugar and flour in a bowl. Stir in the soaked figs and any liquid, the eggs and butter. Spoon into the basin. Cover the pudding with baking paper and foil (see p. 187). Cover the basin with a lid and make a handle with string. Lower the basin into the boiling water, reduce to a fast simmer and cover the saucepan with a tight-fitting lid. Cook for 3$\frac{1}{2}$ hours, checking the water every hour and topping up with boiling water as necessary. The pudding is cooked when a skewer inserted in the centre comes out clean. Leave for 5 minutes before turning out. Serve with custard or cream.

PREPARATION TIME: 40 MINUTES   COOKING TIME: 3 HOURS 40 MINUTES

QUICK STEAMED FRUIT MINCE PUDDING

155 g (5$\frac{1}{2}$ oz/1$\frac{1}{4}$ cups) self-raising flour
$\frac{1}{4}$ teaspoon mixed (pumpkin pie) spice
125 g (4$\frac{1}{2}$ oz) butter, softened
160 g (5$\frac{3}{4}$ oz/$\frac{2}{3}$ cup) caster (superfine) sugar
3 eggs, lightly beaten
60 g (2$\frac{1}{4}$ oz/$\frac{1}{3}$ cup) bottled fruit mince (mincemeat)

SERVES 4

Place a 1 litre (35 fl oz/4 cup) pudding basin (steamed pudding mould) on a trivet or upturned saucer in the base of a large saucepan and pour in enough cold water to come halfway up the side of the basin. Remove the basin and put the water on to boil. Lightly grease the basin with butter and line the base with baking paper.

Sift the flour and mixed spice into a large bowl. Make a well in the centre, add the butter, sugar, beaten eggs and fruit mince and beat until well combined. Spoon the mixture into the basin and level the top. Cover the pudding with baking paper and foil (see p. 187). Cover the basin with the lid and make a handle. Gently lower the basin into the boiling water, cover the saucepan with a tight-fitting lid and cook for 1 hour 45 minutes. Check the water level occasionally and replenish with boiling water when necessary. Leave for 5 minutes before turning onto a plate.

PREPARATION TIME: 20 MINUTES   COOKING TIME: 1 HOUR 45 MINUTES

SAGO PLUM PUDDING WITH RUM BUTTER

65 g (2¼ oz/⅓ cup) sago
250 ml (9 fl oz/1 cup) milk
1 teaspoon bicarbonate of soda (baking soda)
140 g (5 oz/¾ cup) dark brown sugar
160 g (5¾ oz/2 cups) fresh white breadcrumbs
80 g (2¾ oz/½ cup) sultanas (golden raisins)
75 g (2½ oz/½ cup) currants
80 g (2¾ oz/½ cup) dried dates, chopped
2 eggs, lightly beaten
60 g (2¼ oz) unsalted butter, melted and cooled
raspberries, to decorate
blueberries, to decorate
icing (confectioners') sugar, to decorate

RUM BUTTER
125 g (4½ oz) butter, softened
140 g (5 oz/¾ cup) dark brown sugar
80 ml (2½ fl oz/⅓ cup) rum

SERVES 6–8

Combine the sago and milk in a bowl, cover and refrigerate overnight.

Lightly grease a 1.5 litre (52 fl oz/6 cup) pudding basin (steamed pudding mould) with butter and line the base with baking paper. Place the empty basin in a large saucepan on a trivet or upturned saucer and pour in enough cold water to come halfway up the side of the basin. Remove the basin and put the water on to boil.

Transfer the soaked sago and milk to a large bowl and stir in the bicarbonate of soda until dissolved. Stir in the sugar, breadcrumbs, dried fruit, beaten eggs and melted butter and mix well. Spoon into the basin and smooth the surface with wet hands. Cover the pudding (see p. 189).

Cover the basin with the lid and make a string handle. Gently lower the basin into the boiling water, reduce to a fast simmer and cover the saucepan with a tight-fitting lid. Cook for 3½–4 hours, or until a skewer inserted into the centre of the pudding comes out clean. Check the water level every hour and top up with boiling water as necessary.

Carefully remove the pudding basin from the saucepan, remove the coverings and leave for 5 minutes before turning out the pudding onto a large serving plate. Loosen the edges with a palette knife, if necessary. Serve decorated with raspberries and blueberries and lightly dusted with icing sugar. Serve hot with cold rum butter.

For the rum butter, beat together the butter and sugar with electric beaters for about 3–4 minutes, or until light and creamy. Gradually beat in the rum, 1 tablespoon at a time. You can add more rum, to taste. Transfer to a serving dish, cover and refrigerate until required.

PREPARATION TIME: 35 MINUTES +   COOKING TIME: 4 HOURS

NOTE: Sago is the starch extracted from the sago palm. It is dried and formed into balls by pushing through a sieve. It is often called pearl sago and is available from supermarkets or health food stores. It is white when uncooked but goes transparent when cooked.

BAKING

TRADITIONAL MINCE TARTS

FRUIT MINCE

2 large green apples (about 440 g/14 oz), peeled, cored and finely chopped

250 g (9 oz) packet suet mix

345 g (12 oz/1½ cups) soft brown sugar

375 g (13 oz/2⅓ cups) raisins, chopped

240 g (8¾ oz/1½ cups) sultanas (golden raisins)

225 g (8 oz/1½ cups) currants

140 g (5 oz/¾ cup) mixed peel (mixed candied citrus peel)

100 g (3½ oz) slivered almonds, chopped

1 tablespoon mixed (pumpkin pie) spice

½ teaspoon freshly grated nutmeg

½ teaspoon ground cinnamon

2 teaspoons grated orange zest

1 teaspoon grated lemon zest

250 ml (9 fl oz/1 cup) orange juice

125 ml (4 fl oz/½ cup) lemon juice

150 ml (5 fl oz) brandy

PASTRY

800 g (1 lb 12 oz) plain (all-purpose) flour

1 teaspoon caster (superfine) sugar

400 g (14 oz) unsalted butter, chilled, chopped

4 eggs, lightly beaten

4 drops vanilla essence

1 egg white, lightly beaten, to glaze

MAKES 48

Combine all the fruit mince ingredients with 125 ml (4 fl oz/½ cup) of the brandy in a large bowl. Mix thoroughly. Spoon into sterilized, warm jars. Use a skewer to remove air bubbles and to pack the mixture in firmly. Leave a 1.5 cm (⅝ inch) space at the top of the jar and wipe the jar clean with a cloth. Spoon a little brandy over the surface of the mince and seal. Label and date. Set aside for at least 3 weeks, or up to 6 months, before using in pies and tarts. Refrigerate the mince in hot weather.

To make the pastry, in a large bowl, sift together the flour, sugar and a large pinch of salt. Rub the butter into the flour with your fingertips until the mixture resembles fine breadcrumbs. Make a well in the centre and pour in the combined egg, vanilla and 2–3 teaspoons water. Bring the mixture together with a flat-bladed knife or pastry scraper to form a rough ball. If it is slightly sticky, add a little more flour. Turn out onto a lightly floured cool surface, gather into a ball and flatten slightly. Wrap in plastic wrap and chill for 20 minutes.

Separate one-third of the pastry, re-wrap in plastic and return to the fridge. Roll the remaining pastry to 3 mm (⅛ inch) and cut out 48 rounds using a 7 cm (2¾ inch) plain or fluted cutter.

Line four 12-hole, 7 cm (2¾ inch) diameter, shallow tart tins. Fill each with 1 level tablespoon fruit mince. Return to the fridge.

Preheat the oven to 200°C (400°F/Gas 6). Roll out the remaining pastry and cut 48 round shapes for pastry lids using a 6 cm (2½ inch) round cutter. Cut shapes out of the centre of some of the tops if you wish. Gather the scraps and re-roll. Place one on top of each pie and refrigerate for 15 minutes.

Brush with egg white, dust with sugar if desired, and bake for 12–15 minutes.

PREPARATION TIME: 40 MINUTES + REFRIGERATION + 3 WEEKS BOTTLING
COOKING TIME: 15 MINUTES

SPECULAAS

405 g (14¼ oz/3¼ cups) plain (all-purpose) flour
1 teaspoon ground cinnamon
¼ teaspoon freshly grated nutmeg
¼ teaspoon ground cloves
¼ teaspoon ground cardamom
160 g (5¾ oz) unsalted butter, softened
310 g (11 oz/1⅓ cups) soft brown sugar
1 egg
80 ml (2¾ fl oz/⅓ cup) milk
45 g (1½ oz/¼ cup) ground almonds
milk, extra, for glazing

MAKES ABOUT 48

Preheat the oven to 200°C (400°F/Gas 6). Cover baking trays with baking paper. Sift the flour, spices and ¼ teaspoon salt together into a large bowl.

Beat the butter and sugar together in a bowl until pale and creamy. Beat in the egg, mixing well, and then the milk. Fold in the almonds, then the sifted flour and spices and mix well. Wrap in plastic and refrigerate for 45 minutes.

Divide the mixture into four portions and roll out each portion on a lightly floured surface to 4 mm (⅛ inch) thick. Cut into shapes using Christmas-theme cutters (stars, trees, candy canes or bells). Place on the baking trays, leaving room for spreading. Brush with milk and bake for 12 minutes, or until light brown. Repeat with the remaining dough, returning any scraps to the refrigerator to chill before re-rolling. Cool the biscuits on wire racks. When cold, store in airtight containers.

PREPARATION TIME: 20 MINUTES +   COOKING TIME: 12 MINUTES

GINGER PECAN BISCOTTI

100 g (3½ oz/1 cup) pecans
2 eggs
155 g (5½ oz/⅔ cup) soft brown sugar
125 g (4½ oz/1 cup) self-raising flour
90 g (3¼ oz/¾ cup) plain (all-purpose) flour
100 g (3½ oz) glacé (candied) ginger, finely chopped

MAKES ABOUT 20

Preheat the oven to 160°C (315°F/Gas 2–3). Spread the pecans on a baking tray and bake for 10–12 minutes, or until fragrant. Tip onto a chopping board to cool, then chop. Cover the baking tray with baking paper.

Put the eggs and sugar in a bowl and beat with electric beaters until pale and creamy. Sift the flours into the bowl and add the nuts and ginger. Mix to a soft dough, then place on the tray and shape into a 9 x 23 cm (3½ x 9 inch) loaf. Bake for 45 minutes, or until lightly golden. Transfer to a wire rack to cool for about 20 minutes, then cut into 1 cm (½ inch) slices with a large serrated bread knife. It will be crumbly on the edges, so work slowly and, if possible, try to hold the sides as you cut. Arrange the slices on baking trays and bake again for about 10 minutes on each side. Cool before storing in an airtight container.

PREPARATION TIME: 30 MINUTES   COOKING TIME: 1 HOUR 20 MINUTES

INDIVIDUAL BOURBON CHRISTMAS CAKES

60 g (2¼ oz/¼ cup) chopped glacé (candied) apricots
110 g (3¾ oz/½ cup) chopped glacé (candied) pineapple
100 g (3½ oz/½ cup) chopped glacé (candied) figs
320 g (11¼ oz/2 cups) raisins, chopped
250 g (9 oz/1⅔ cups) currants
185 ml (6 fl oz/¾ cup) bourbon
250 g (9 oz) unsalted butter, chopped
230 g (8½ oz/1 cup) dark brown sugar
180 g (6½ oz/½ cup) treacle
4 eggs
310 g (11 oz/2½ cups) pecans, chopped
185 g (6½ oz/1½ cups) plain (all-purpose) flour
60 g (2¼ oz/½ cup) self-raising flour
2 teaspoons ground nutmeg
2 teaspoons ground ginger
2 teaspoons ground cinnamon
6 tablespoons bourbon, extra

HOLLY LEAVES AND BERRIES
60 g (2¼ oz) ready-made almond icing
pure icing (confectioners') sugar
green and red food colouring

SOFT ICING-COVERED CAKES
105 g (3½ oz/⅓ cup) apricot jam (jelly)
1.2 kg (2 lb 12 oz) soft icing (frosting)
pure icing (confectioners') sugar
thin ribbon, to decorate

ROYAL ICING-COVERED CAKES
1 egg white
250 g (9 oz/2 cups) pure icing (confectioners') sugar, sifted
2–3 teaspoons lemon juice

MAKES 12

Cut the glacé fruits and raisins into small pieces. Place in a bowl with the currants and bourbon and mix. Cover and leave to soak overnight.

Preheat the oven to 150°C (300°F/Gas 2). Lightly grease twelve 250 ml (9 fl oz/1 cup) muffin holes and line the bases with a circle of baking paper. Beat the butter, sugar and treacle in a bowl. Add the eggs, one at a time, beating well after each addition. Transfer to a bowl, stir in the soaked fruit mixture, pecans and the sifted dry ingredients and mix. Spoon the mixture evenly into the tins, and smooth the surface. Bake for 1–1¼ hours, or until a skewer inserted into the centre comes out clean. Cover the top of the cakes with foil if over-browning. Brush the tops of the cakes with half the extra bourbon while hot, cover with baking paper, then seal with foil and cool in the tins before turning out. Brush with the remaining bourbon, wrap firmly in plastic and leave for two weeks before decorating. When decorating, the base will become the top.

To make the holly leaves, knead 50 g (1¾ oz) of the almond icing until it is soft. Roll out on a surface dusted with icing sugar until very thin. Cut out the leaves using a cutter or template. Pinch the leaves in half, open out and press the edges gently to curl in different directions. Dry on baking paper. Brush the edges with green food colouring. Knead a little red colouring into the remaining almond icing and roll into balls to make berries. Paint or roll the berries in colouring to coat. Allow to dry.

To make the soft icing-covered cakes, melt the jam until runny, strain and brush some all over each cake. Roll out 100 g (3½ oz) of the soft icing on a surface dusted with icing sugar until large enough to cover one cake. Place the icing over the cake and ease over the side, pressing lightly, then trim from around the base. Mix together a little icing sugar and water into a smooth paste. Wrap a ribbon around the base of the cake and seal with a little paste. Use the paste to secure two holly leaves and berries to the top. Repeat with remaining cakes and icing.

For the royal icing-covered cakes, lightly beat the egg white. Gradually add the icing sugar, beating to a smooth paste. Add the lemon juice until slightly runny. Spread a tablespoon of icing over each cake, using a palette knife to smooth and letting some drizzle down the sides. Secure holly leaves and berries on the top just before the icing sets.

PREPARATION TIME: 40 MINUTES +   COOKING TIME: 1 HOUR 15 MINUTES

GALETTE DES ROIS

2 x 375 g (12 oz) blocks ready-made puff pastry, thawed
75 g (2½ oz/¾ cup) ground almonds
90 g (3¼ oz/⅓ cup) caster (superfine) sugar or vanilla sugar
1 tablespoon cornflour (cornstarch)
1 teaspoon finely grated orange zest
100 g (3½ oz) unsalted butter, softened
3 egg yolks
½ teaspoon almond essence
1 tablespoon rum or kirsch
1 dried haricot bean or ceramic token
1 egg, lightly beaten, for glazing

MAKES 1

Roll out one block of pastry on a lightly floured surface to 5 mm (¼ inch) thick and cut into a 22 cm (9 inch) circle. Repeat with the other block of pastry. Line a baking tray with baking paper and top with one of the circles.

In a bowl, combine the almonds, sugar, cornflour and zest. Add the butter, egg yolks, essence and rum and mix well. Spread over the pastry on the tray, poking in the bean or token and leaving a 2 cm (¾ inch) rim. Brush the rim with some beaten egg, taking care not to brush the cut edges as this will prevent the pastry from puffing.

Place the second circle of puff pastry over the first, pressing gently around the edge to seal. Using a sharp knife, make swirling patterns from the centre, fanning outwards in the pastry, taking care not to cut all the way through. Brush the top with beaten egg and refrigerate for 30 minutes. Preheat the oven to 200°C (400°F/Gas 6). Bake for 30–35 minutes, or until well puffed and golden. Serve warm or cold. Remember to tell everyone about the bean or token in the filling.

PREPARATION TIME: 25 MINUTES +   COOKING TIME: 35 MINUTES

UKRAINIAN HONEY CAKE

375 g (13 oz/3 cups) self-raising flour
250 g (9 oz/1 cup) sugar
2 teaspoons ground ginger
1 teaspoon ground cloves
1 teaspoon ground cinnamon
1 teaspoon bicarbonate of soda (baking soda)
1 teaspoon vanilla essence
2 eggs, lightly beaten
350 g (12 oz/1 cup) honey
250 ml (9 fl oz/1 cup) sunflower oil

MAKES 1

Preheat the oven to 170°C (325°F/Gas 3). Lightly grease a 24 x 9 x 10 cm (9 x 3½ x 4 inch) loaf (bar) tin and line the base with baking paper.

Sift the flour into a large bowl, make a well in the centre and add all the remaining ingredients. Pour in 250 ml (9 fl oz/1 cup) hot water, stir thoroughly to mix, then beat until quite smooth. Spoon the mixture into the prepared loaf tin and lightly tap the tin on the bench to remove any air pockets. Bake for 1 hour 20 minutes, or until a skewer inserted into the centre comes out clean. If the cake starts to brown too much, cover loosely with foil halfway through cooking. Leave to cool in the tin for 20 minutes, then invert onto a wire rack and cool completely.

PREPARATION TIME: 15 MINUTES   COOKING TIME: 1 HOUR 20 MINUTES

PANETTONE

90 g (3¼ oz/½ cup) mixed peel (mixed candied citrus peel)
80 g (2¾ oz/½ cup) sultanas (golden raisins)
1 teaspoon grated lemon zest
1 teaspoon grated orange zest
1 tablespoon brandy or rum
7 g (¼ oz) sachet dried yeast
220 ml (7½ fl oz) warm milk
60 g (2¼ oz/¼ cup) caster (superfine) sugar
400 g (14 oz/3¼ cups) white strong flour
2 eggs
1 teaspoon vanilla essence
150 g (5½ oz) unsalted butter, softened
20 g (½ oz) unsalted butter, melted, to glaze

MAKES 1

Put the peel, sultanas and grated zest in a small bowl. Add the alcohol, mix well and set aside.

Put the yeast, warm milk and 1 teaspoon sugar in a small bowl and leave in a warm place for 10–15 minutes, or until foamy. Sift 200 g (7 oz) flour and ½ teaspoon salt into a large bowl, make a well in the centre and add the yeast mixture. Mix together with a large metal spoon to form a soft dough. Cover the bowl and leave to 'sponge' and rise in a warm place for 45 minutes, or until frothy and risen.

Add the eggs, remaining sugar and vanilla and mix. Add the butter and stir until well combined. Stir in the remaining flour and mix well. Knead well on a floured surface until the dough is smooth and elastic. You may need to add up to 60 g (2¼ oz/½ cup) flour to the dough as you knead. Place the dough in a lightly greased bowl, cover with plastic wrap and leave in a warm place for 1½–2 hours, or until doubled.

Lightly grease a 15 cm (6 inch) round cake tin and line the base and side with a double thickness of baking paper, ensuring the collar extends above the rim of the tin by 10 cm (4 inches).

Knock back the dough and turn out onto a floured work surface. Roll into a 30 x 20 cm (12 x 8 inch) rectangle. Drain the fruit mixture and spread half the fruit over the surface of the dough. Fold over the short edges like an envelope to cover the fruit. Roll again and repeat the process to incorporate all the fruit. Gently knead the dough for 2–3 minutes and shape into a neat ball. Place in the tin, brush with the melted butter, then slash a cross on the top with a sharp knife and leave to rise again in a warm place for 45 minutes, or until doubled in size.

Preheat the oven to 190°C (375°F/Gas 5). Bake for 50 minutes, or until golden brown and a skewer inserted into the centre comes out clean. Leave in the tin for 5 minutes, then transfer to a wire rack to cool.

PREPARATION TIME: 30 MINUTES + RISING   COOKING TIME: 50 MINUTES

NOTE: This yeast cake is a speciality of Milan but is enjoyed throughout Italy at festive times such as Christmas and Easter.

CINNAMON STARS

2 egg whites
280 g (10 oz/2¼ cups) icing
(confectioners') sugar
145 g (5 oz/1½ cups) ground almonds
1½ tablespoons ground cinnamon

MAKES ABOUT 30

Beat the egg whites lightly with a wooden spoon in a large bowl. Gradually stir in the sifted icing sugar to form a smooth paste. Remove 100 g (3½ oz/⅓ cup), cover and set aside. Add the almonds and cinnamon to the remaining icing and gently press together with your hands. Add 1 teaspoon water if the mixture is too dry. Press together well before adding any water as the warmth of your hands will soften the mixture.

Lightly dust a work surface with icing sugar and roll out the mixture to about 3 mm (⅛ inch) thick. Spread with a thin layer of the reserved icing. Leave, uncovered, at room temperature for 30–35 minutes, or until the icing has set. Preheat the oven to 150°C (300°F/Gas 2). Cut out shapes using a star cutter (about 5 cm/2 inches across from point to point). Dip the cutter in icing sugar to help prevent sticking. Place the stars on a baking tray covered with baking paper and cook for 10 minutes, or until just firm. Turn the tray around after 5 minutes. Cool on the tray. Store in an airtight container for up to 2 weeks.

PREPARATION TIME: 15 MINUTES   COOKING TIME: 10 MINUTES PER BATCH

SCOTTISH SHORTBREAD

250 g (9 oz) butter, softened
160 g (5¾ oz/⅔ cup) caster
(superfine) sugar
210 g (7½ oz/1⅔ cups) plain
(all-purpose) flour
90 g (3¼ oz/½ cup) rice flour
1 teaspoon sugar, for sprinkling

MAKES ONE 28 CM (11 INCH) ROUND

Preheat the oven to 160°C (315°F/Gas 2–3). Brush a 28 cm (11¼ inch) round pizza tray with melted butter or oil. Line with baking paper. Beat the butter and sugar with electric beaters in a small bowl until light and creamy. Transfer to a large bowl and add the sifted flours. Mix to a soft dough with a flat-bladed knife. Lift onto a lightly floured surface and knead for 30 seconds, or until smooth.

Transfer to the pizza tray and press into a 25 cm (10 inch) round. Pinch and flute the edge decoratively with your fingers. Prick the surface lightly with a fork and mark into 16 segments with a sharp knife. Sprinkle with sugar and bake on the middle shelf for 35 minutes, or until firm and lightly golden. Cool on the tray.

PREPARATION TIME: 15 MINUTES   COOKING TIME: 35 MINUTES

FROSTED FRUIT CAKE

640 g (1 lb 7 oz/4 cups) sultanas (golden raisins)
480 g (1 lb 1 oz/3 cups) raisins, chopped
300 g (10$\frac{1}{2}$ oz/2 cups) currants
265 g (9$\frac{1}{4}$ oz/1$\frac{1}{4}$ cups) glacé (candied) cherries, quartered
250 ml (9 fl oz/1 cup) brandy or rum
250 g (9 oz) unsalted butter, chopped, softened
230 g (8 oz/1 cup) dark brown sugar
2 tablespoons apricot jam (jelly)
2 tablespoons treacle or golden syrup
1 tablespoon grated lemon or orange zest
4 eggs
340 g (11$\frac{3}{4}$ oz/2$\frac{3}{4}$ cups) plain (all-purpose) flour
1 teaspoon mixed (pumpkin pie) spice
1 teaspoon ground cinnamon
1 teaspoon ground ginger
1 tablespoon brandy or rum, extra

DECORATIONS
selection of seasonal fruits such as white and dark cherries, small bunches of red, white and black currants, apricots, tiny plums or pears
1 egg white
caster (superfine) sugar

ICING
1 egg white
1-3 teaspoons lemon juice
125 g (4$\frac{1}{2}$ oz/1 cup) pure icing (confectioners') sugar, sifted

MAKES 1

Put the fruit in a large bowl with the brandy and leave to soak overnight. Preheat the oven to 150°C (300°F/Gas 2). Grease and line an oval cake tin 18 x 25 cm (7 x 10 inch), or a 23 cm (9 inch) round cake tin.

Beat the butter and sugar in a small bowl with electric beaters until just combined. Beat in the jam, treacle and zest. Add the eggs one at a time, beating well after each addition. Transfer to a large bowl.

Stir the fruit and the combined sifted flour and spices alternately into the mixture. Spoon into the tin, tap the tin on the bench to remove any air bubbles and smooth the surface with wet fingers. Wrap newspaper around the outside of the tin. Sit the tin on several layers of newspaper in the oven and bake for 3$\frac{1}{4}$-3$\frac{1}{2}$ hours, or until a skewer inserted into the centre comes out clean. Drizzle with the extra brandy while hot. Cover the top with baking paper, cover tightly with foil and wrap the tin in a tea towel (dish towel) until the cake is completely cold.

Remove from the tin and store in an airtight container or wrapped in plastic wrap for up to 8 months.

Wash the fruit to be used for decorating several hours in advance so it is completely dry. Line a tray with paper towels. Place the egg white in a shallow bowl and whisk until just foamy. Put some caster sugar on a large plate and, working with one portion of fruit at a time, brush the egg white lightly all over the fruit. Sprinkle the sugar over the fruit, shaking off any excess and leave to dry on the paper-covered tray for about 1-2 hours, depending on the humidity. Frost more fruit than you think you will need so you have a good selection.

For the icing, whisk the egg white until just foamy, beat in 1 teaspoon of lemon juice and then gradually beat in the icing (confectioners') sugar, beating well after each addition. The icing should be thick and white — add a little more lemon juice if necessary, but don't make it too runny. Place the fruit cake on a serving plate and, working quickly, pour the icing over the top. Using a palette knife, smooth the icing to the edge of the cake, allowing it to run slowly down the side of the cake. Leave for at least 10 minutes to let the icing set a little before arranging the frosted fruits on the top. The iced cake will keep for up to a month.

PREPARATION TIME: 30 MINUTES +   COOKING TIME: 3 HOURS 30 MINUTES

LIGHT FRUIT CAKE

185 g (6½ oz) unsalted butter, softened
115 g (4 oz/½ cup) caster (superfine) sugar
3 eggs
160 g (5½ oz/1 cup) sultanas (golden raisins)
100 g (3½ oz/²/₃ cup) currants
60 g (2¼ oz/¼ cup) chopped glacé (candied) apricots
45 g (1½ oz/¼ cup) chopped glacé (candied) figs
240 g (7½ oz/1 cup) chopped glacé (candied) cherries, plus extra to decorate
80 g (2¾ oz/½ cup) macadamia nuts, coarsely chopped
185 g (6½ oz/1½ cups) plain (all-purpose) flour
60 g (2¼ oz/½ cup) self-raising flour
125 ml (4 fl oz/½ cup) milk
1 tablespoon sweet sherry

MAKES 1

Preheat the oven to 160°C (315°F/Gas 2–3). Grease and line a deep 20 cm (8 inch) round or 18 cm (7 inch) square cake tin.

Cream the butter and sugar in a bowl until just combined. Add the eggs, one at a time, beating well after each addition. Transfer the mixture to a bowl and stir in the fruit and nuts. Sift in half the flours and half the milk, stir to combine, then stir in the remaining flours and milk, and the sherry. Spoon into the prepared tin and tap the tin on the bench to remove any air bubbles. Smooth the surface with wet fingers and decorate the top with nuts or cherries, or both. Wrap the outside of the tin. Sit the tin on layers of newspaper in the oven and bake for 1¾–2 hours, or until a skewer inserted into the centre comes out clean. The top may need to be covered with a sheet of baking paper if it colours too much.

Remove from the oven, remove the top baking paper and wrap the tin in a tea towel (dish towel) until cool. Remove the paper tin lining and store in an airtight container. Keeps for up to 2 weeks.

PREPARATION TIME: 30 MINUTES   COOKING TIME: 2 HOURS

PANFORTE

100 g (3½ oz/²/₃ cup) blanched almonds
105 g (3½ oz/¾ cup) roasted hazelnuts
95 g (3¼ oz/½ cup) mixed peel (mixed candied citrus peel), chopped
100 g (3½ oz/½ cup) chopped glacé (candied) pineapple
30 g (1 oz/¼ cup) unsweetened cocoa powder
60 g (2¼ oz/½ cup) plain (all-purpose) flour
½ teaspoon ground cinnamon
¼ teaspoon mixed (pumpkin pie) spice
90 g (3¼ oz/⅓ cup) sugar
115 g (4 oz/⅓ cup) honey
icing (confectioners') sugar, for dusting

MAKES 1

Line a 20 cm (8 inch) spring-form cake tin with baking paper and grease well with butter. Toast the almonds under a hot grill (broiler) until brown, then cool. Put the nuts in a bowl with the peel, pineapple, cocoa powder, flour and spices and toss. Preheat the oven to 150°C (300°F/Gas 2).

Put the sugar and honey in a saucepan and melt over low heat. Cook the syrup until a little of it dropped into cold water forms a soft ball when moulded between your finger and thumb. The colour will turn from golden to brown. Pour the syrup into the nut mixture and mix well, working fast before it stiffens too much. Spoon straight into the tin, press firmly and smooth the surface. Bake for 35 minutes.

Cool in the tin. Remove from the tin and leave to cool completely. Dust the top heavily with icing sugar before serving.

PREPARATION TIME: 20 MINUTES   COOKING TIME: 40 MINUTES

SAFFRON BUNS

2 x 7 g (¼ oz) sachets dry yeast
500 ml (17 fl oz/2 cups) milk
½ teaspoon saffron threads
150 g (5½ oz) unsalted butter, chopped
875 g (1 lb 15 oz/7 cups) white strong flour
1 teaspoon salt
160 g (5½ oz/²⁄₃ cup) sugar
160 g (5½ oz/1 cup) raisins
2 eggs, lightly beaten

MAKES 16

Combine the yeast with 125 ml (4 fl oz/½ cup) warm milk and the saffron in a small bowl. Set aside for 5 minutes, or until foamy. Melt the butter in a small saucepan, add the saffron and remaining milk and stir over low heat until warm. Remove from the heat and cover.

Sift the flour into a large bowl, stir in the frothy yeast, salt, sugar and half the raisins, then make a well in the centre. Add the just-warm saffron milk mixture and one of the eggs. Mix with a flat-bladed knife, using a cutting action, until the mixture comes together to form a soft dough.

Turn out the dough onto a lightly floured work surface and knead for 5–7 minutes, or until the dough is smooth. Place the dough in a large, lightly oiled bowl, cover with plastic wrap or a damp tea towel, and leave for 1–1½ hours in a warm place or until doubled in size.

Turn out the dough onto a lightly floured work surface and knead for 5 minutes. Cut into 16 portions. Roll each portion into a sausage shape about 20 cm (8 inches) long and form each into an 'S' shape. Place on a greased baking tray. Cover and stand in a warm place for 30 minutes, or until doubled in size. Preheat the oven to 200°C (400°F/Gas 6).

Brush with the remaining beaten egg and decorate with the remaining raisins, placing them gently into the 'S' shape, being careful not to deflate the buns. Bake for 10 minutes, or until the tops are brown and the buns feel hollow when tapped underneath. Transfer to a wire rack to cool. Serve warm or cold, plain or buttered.

PREPARATION TIME: 30 MINUTES + RISING   COOKING TIME: 10 MINUTES

FRUIT CAKE

250 g (9 oz) softened unsalted butter
230 g (8 oz/1 cup) soft brown sugar
2 teaspoons finely grated orange zest
2 teaspoons finely grated lemon zest
4 eggs
250 g (9 oz/2 cups) plain
(all-purpose) flour, sifted
60 g (2¼ oz/½ cup) self-raising
flour, sifted
whole blanched almonds, to decorate

MAKES 1

Preheat the oven to 150°C (300°F/Gas 2). Grease and line a 23 cm (9 inch) round or square cake tin.

Beat the butter, soft brown sugar and orange and lemon zests in a bowl with electric beaters until just combined. Add the eggs, one at a time, beating well after each addition. Transfer to a bowl and stir in half of the soaked fruit mix alternately with the plain flour and the self-raising flour. Mix well, then spread evenly into the tin and tap the tin on the bench to remove any air bubbles. Dip your fingers in water and level the surface.

Decorate the top of the cake with whole blanched almonds in a pattern. Sit the cake on several layers of newspaper on the oven shelf and bake for 3¼–3½ hours, or until a skewer comes out clean. Cover the top with baking paper, seal firmly with foil, then wrap the cake and tin in a clean tea towel (dish towel) and leave to cool.

PREPARATION TIME: 20 MINUTES   COOKING TIME: 3 HOURS 30 MINUTES

KOURABIETHES

250 g (9 oz) butter, softened
125 g (4½ oz/1 cup) icing (confectioners')
sugar
1½ teaspoons vanilla essence
½ teaspoon finely grated orange zest
1 egg yolk
1½ tablespoons brandy
310 g (11 oz/2½ cups) plain
(all-purpose) flour
1 teaspoon baking powder
30 g (1 oz/⅓ cup) ground almonds
40 g (1½ oz/⅓ cup) slivered almonds,
finely chopped
2 tablespoons orange flower water
185 g (6½ oz/1½ cups) icing
(confectioners') sugar, extra, for dusting

MAKES ABOUT 40

Preheat the oven to 160°C (315°F/Gas 2–3). Line two baking trays with baking paper.

Beat the butter, icing sugar, vanilla essence and orange zest in a bowl with electric beaters until light and creamy. Gradually add the egg yolk and brandy and beat until combined.

Sift the flour and baking powder into a large bowl, stir in the ground and chopped slivered almonds, then stir into the butter mixture. Form walnut-sized pieces into crescent shapes and place on the trays, leaving a little room for spreading. Bake for 20 minutes, or until just lightly coloured. Cool for 5 minutes, then brush with the orange flower water. Roll in icing sugar to coat and set aside on wire racks to cool. When cool, dredge the remaining icing sugar heavily over the top of the kourabiethes.

PREPARATION TIME: 20 MINUTES   COOKING TIME: 20 MINUTES

FRESH FRUIT MINCE TARTS

215 g (7½ oz/1¾ cups) plain (all-purpose) flour
150 g (5½ oz) butter, chilled and chopped
80 g (2¾ oz/¾ cup) ground hazelnuts
2 tablespoons caster (superfine) sugar
1–2 tablespoons iced water
icing (confectioners') sugar, for dusting

FILLING
115 g (4 oz/¾ cup) blueberries
200 g (7 oz/1 cup) peeled, finely chopped apple
80 g (2¾ oz/½ cup) raisins, chopped
75 g (2½ oz/½ cup) currants
80 g (2¾ oz/½ cup) sultanas (golden raisins)
30 g (1 oz/¼ cup) slivered almonds, toasted
60 g (2¼ oz/¼ cup) caster (superfine) sugar
2 tablespoons mixed peel (mixed candied citrus peel)
125 ml (4 fl oz/½ cup) brandy
1 teaspoon grated lemon zest
½ teaspoon mixed (pumpkin pie) spice
½ teaspoon ground ginger

MAKES 24

To make the pastry, sift the flour into a large bowl and rub in the butter with your fingertips until the mixture resembles fine breadcrumbs. Stir in the nuts and sugar. Make a well and mix in the water with a flat-bladed knife until the mixture comes together in beads. Gather into a ball and turn out onto a lightly floured surface. Press into a ball and flatten slightly into a disc. Cover with plastic wrap and chill for 30 minutes.

Preheat the oven to 180°C (350°F/Gas 4). Roll out the dough between sheets of baking paper to 3 mm (⅛ inch) thick. Using a 7 cm (2¾ inch) round pastry cutter, cut 24 pastry rounds and line two deep 12-hole tartlet pans with the rounds. Line each pastry case with baking paper and fill with baking beads. Bake for 10 minutes, remove the paper and beads and bake for another 10 minutes.

Meanwhile, press together the pastry scraps and roll to 3 mm (⅛ inch) thick. Using 4.5 cm (1¾ inch) star-, bell- or holly-shaped cutters, cut 24 shapes from the pastry for the tart lids.

To make the filling, put all the ingredients in a saucepan and simmer, stirring, for 5–10 minutes, or until thick and pulpy. Cool slightly. Divide among the pastry cases, then top each with a pastry lid. Bake for 20 minutes, or until the lids are golden. Leave in the pans for 5 minutes before transferring to a wire rack to cool. Dust with sifted icing sugar before serving. Store in an airtight container for up to a week.

PREPARATION TIME: 1 HOUR +   COOKING TIME: 50 MINUTES

SPICED GINGERBREAD

140 g (5 oz) unsalted butter, softened
115 g (4 oz/½ cup) dark brown sugar
90 g (3 oz/¼ cup) treacle
1 egg
250 g (9 oz/2 cups) plain (all-purpose) flour
30 g (1 oz/¼ cup) self-raising flour
3 teaspoons ground ginger
2 teaspoons ground cinnamon
¾ teaspoon ground cloves
¾ teaspoon freshly grated nutmeg
1 teaspoon bicarbonate of soda (baking soda)

ICING
1 egg white
½ teaspoon lemon juice
125 g (4½ oz/1 cup) icing (confectioners') sugar, sifted
assorted food colourings

MAKES ABOUT 36

Lightly grease two baking trays. Beat the butter and sugar in a bowl with electric beaters until light and creamy, then beat in the treacle and egg. Fold in the combined sifted flours, spices and bicarbonate of soda. Turn out onto a lightly floured surface and knead for 2–3 minutes, or until smooth. Cover with plastic wrap and chill for 10 minutes.

Divide the dough in half and roll out between two sheets of baking paper to 4 mm (¼ inch) thick. Lay on the trays and chill for 15 minutes. Preheat the oven to 180°C (350°F/Gas 4). Cut out the dough using a 7 cm (2¾ inch) heart-shaped cutter. Using a sharp knife, cut out a 1 cm (½ inch) hole at the top of each shape. Place on the trays and bake for 10 minutes. Remove from the oven and stand for 5 minutes before transferring to a wire rack. When the biscuits are cold, decorate with icing.

To make the icing, whisk the egg white until foamy. Add the lemon juice and sugar and stir until glossy. Tint the icing any colour you want, then spoon into paper piping bags. When decorated, leave the icing to set.

PREPARATION TIME: 45 MINUTES +   COOKING TIME: 10 MINUTES PER BATCH

CHOCOLATE SHORTBREADS

185 g (6 oz/1½ cups) plain (all-purpose) flour
40 g (1½ oz/⅓ cup) unsweetened cocoa powder
85 g (3 oz/¾ cup) icing (confectioners') sugar
225 g (8 oz) unsalted butter, chopped
2 egg yolks
1 teaspoon vanilla essence
250 ml (9 fl oz/1 cup) pouring cream, whipped
250 g (9 oz) strawberries, quartered

BERRY SAUCE
250 g (9 oz) fresh strawberries
1 tablespoon caster (superfine) sugar

SERVES 6

Preheat the oven to 210°C (415°F/Gas 6–7). Line two baking trays with baking paper. Sift the flour, cocoa and icing sugar into a bowl. Rub in the butter until the mixture resembles breadcrumbs. Add the yolks and vanilla and mix. Turn out onto a floured surface and gather together into a ball. Roll the pastry between two layers of baking paper to 5 mm (¼ inch) thick. Using a 7 cm (2¾ inch) fluted round cutter, cut 18 rounds from the pastry. Place on the trays and bake for 8 minutes. Transfer to a wire rack to cool. Place a biscuit on a plate, top with cream and strawberries. Top with a second biscuit, cream and strawberries, then a third biscuit. Repeat to make another five stacks. Dust each with sifted cocoa and icing sugar.

To make the sauce, process the strawberries and sugar until smooth and stir in 1–2 tablespoons water. Serve with the shortbreads.

PREPARATION TIME: 25 MINUTES +   COOKING TIME: 10 MINUTES

CHRISTOPSOMO

1 tablespoon sesame seeds
7 g ($^1/_4$ oz) sachet dry yeast
2 teaspoons sugar
310 g (11 oz/2$^1/_2$ cups) plain (all-purpose) flour
2 teaspoons whole aniseeds
2 tablespoons unsalted butter, melted
125 ml (4 fl oz/$^1/_2$ cup) milk, warmed
1 tablespoon ouzo
1 egg, lightly beaten
2 tablespoons chopped walnuts
1 tablespoon whole blanched almonds, chopped
4 dried figs, chopped
1 teaspoon sesame seeds, extra
2 tablespoons honey

MAKES 1

Grease a 20 cm (8 inch) round cake tin lightly with oil. Sprinkle the sesame seeds over the base and side of the tin.

Place the yeast, sugar and 90 ml (3 fl oz) warm water in a small bowl and leave in a warm place until foamy. (If the yeast doesn't foam, it is dead and you will have to start again.)

Sift the flour into a large bowl, add the aniseeds and stir to combine. Make a well in the centre and add the yeast mixture and combined butter, milk and ouzo. Mix together to form a soft dough, then turn out onto a lightly floured surface and knead for about 10 minutes, until smooth and elastic.

Place the dough in a large greased bowl. Cover and leave in a warm place for 45–60 minutes, or until the dough has doubled. Turn out the dough onto a floured surface and knead until smooth. Break off a small portion of dough about the size of a lime and reserve. This portion will be used for decorating the bread.

Shape the larger piece of dough into a round to fit in the cake tin. Brush lightly all over with some of the beaten egg. Roll the reserved ball of dough into two thin sausage shapes and form an equal-armed cross on the top of the dough, brushing with a little more beaten egg. Arrange the nuts and figs on top of the dough and sprinkle with extra sesame seeds. Cover and leave in a warm place for about 45 minutes, or until the dough has doubled in size.

Preheat the oven to 190ºC (375°F/Gas 5). Bake the bread for 45 minutes, or until it is golden brown and sounds hollow when tapped on the base. Cover loosely with foil if the top is over-browning. Turn onto a wire cake rack and brush with honey while still hot.

PREPARATION TIME: 30 MINUTES + PROVING   COOKING TIME: 45 MINUTES

NOTE: This rich, sweet bread has a slightly denser texture than normal bread.

CHOCOLATE PFEFFERNUSSE

200 ml (7 fl oz) honey
100 ml (3½ fl oz) treacle
155 g (5½ oz/⅔ cup) soft brown sugar
150 g (5½ oz) unsalted butter
500 g (1 lb 2 oz/4 cups) plain (all-purpose) flour
60 g (2¼ oz/½ cup) cocoa powder
1 teaspoon baking powder
½ teaspoon bicarbonate of soda (baking soda)
1 teaspoon ground white pepper
1 teaspoon ground cinnamon
½ teaspoon freshly grated nutmeg
100 g (3½ oz/⅔ cup) almonds, chopped
1 teaspoon finely grated lemon zest
45 g (1½ oz/¼ cup) mixed peel (mixed candied citrus peel)
2 eggs, lightly beaten
300 g (10½ oz) dark chocolate, chopped

MAKES 65

Cover baking trays with baking paper. Heat the honey, treacle, brown sugar and butter in a saucepan over medium heat and bring to the boil. Remove from the heat and set aside to cool. Sift the flour, cocoa, baking powder, bicarbonate of soda, spices and ¼ teaspoon salt into a large bowl. Stir in the almonds, lemon zest and mixed peel. Make a well in the centre. Pour in the honey mixture and the eggs and mix. Cover and refrigerate for 2 hours. Preheat the oven to 180°C (350°F/Gas 4).

Roll level tablespoons of the dough into balls. Place on the trays. Bake for 12–15 minutes, until firm to the touch. Allow to cool.

To decorate, put the chocolate in a heatproof bowl. Bring a saucepan of water to the boil, then remove from the heat. Sit the bowl over the pan, making sure the base of the bowl doesn't sit in the water. Stir occasionally until the chocolate melts. Dip the tops of the biscuits in chocolate (up to the base), allow excess to drain off, then place on baking paper to set.

PREPARATION TIME: 50 MINUTES + COOKING TIME: 15 MINUTES PER TRAY

STOLLEN

80 ml (2¾ fl oz/⅓ cup) lukewarm milk
2 teaspoons sugar
7 g (¼ oz) sachet dried yeast
125 g (4½ oz) unsalted butter, softened
85 g (3 oz/⅓ cup) caster (superfine) sugar
1 egg
2 teaspoons vanilla essence
½ teaspoon ground cinnamon
375 g (12 oz/3 cups) plain (all-purpose) flour
80 g (2¾ oz/½ cup) raisins
75 g (2½ oz/½ cup) currants
95 g (3 oz/½ cup) mixed peel (mixed candied citrus peel)
60 g (2¼ oz/½ cup) slivered almonds
30 g (1 oz) butter, melted
icing (confectioners') sugar, for dusting

MAKES 1

Combine the milk, sugar and yeast with 80 ml (2¾ fl oz/⅓ cup) warm water in a bowl and leave for 10 minutes. Beat the butter and sugar with electric beaters until creamy, then add the egg and vanilla essence. Add the yeast mixture, cinnamon and almost all the flour and mix to a soft dough. Turn out onto a floured surface and knead for 10 minutes, or until smooth. Put in an oiled bowl, cover with plastic wrap and leave for 1 hour 45 minutes. Preheat the oven to 180°C (350°F/Gas 4). Lightly grease a baking tray. Put the dough onto a floured work surface and punch it to expel the air. Press it out to a thickness of 1.5 cm (⅝ inch). Sprinkle over the fruit and nuts, then knead. Shape into an oval 18 x 30 cm (7 x 12 inches). Fold in half lengthways, then press down to flatten, with the fold slightly off centre on top of the loaf. Place on the tray and bake for 40 minutes, or until golden. Brush with the butter. Cool, then dust with icing sugar.

PREPARATION TIME: 30 MINUTES + COOKING TIME: 40 MINUTES

MAKES 1

Chocolate pfeffernusse

BLACK BUN

310 g (11 oz/2½ cups) plain
(all-purpose) flour
½ teaspoon baking powder
150 g (5½ oz) butter, chilled and grated
1 egg, beaten

FILLING
90 g (3¼ oz/¾ cup) plain
(all-purpose) flour
½ teaspoon freshly grated nutmeg
½ teaspoon ground coriander
½ teaspoon mixed (pumpkin pie) spice
1 teaspoon ground cinnamon
1 teaspoon ground ginger
115 g (4 oz/½ cup) soft brown sugar
590 g (1 lb 5 oz/3⅔ cups) raisins,
chopped
240 g (8½ oz/1½ cups) sultanas (golden
raisins)
350 g (12 oz/2⅓ cups) currants
95 g (3¼ oz/½ cup) mixed peel (mixed
candied citrus peel)
100 g (3½ oz/⅔ cup) blanched almonds,
chopped
2 teaspoons finely grated lemon zest
2 eggs
2 tablespoons brandy
3 tablespoons treacle
2 tablespoons milk

MAKES 1

Grease a 24 cm (9 inch) spring-form cake tin. Sift the flour, baking powder and ¼ teaspoon salt into a bowl. Mix the butter into the flour with your fingertips. Make a well, add up to 80 ml (2¾ fl oz/⅓ cup) water and mix with a flat-bladed knife, using a cutting action, until the mixture comes together in clumps (you may need extra water). Gather together and lift onto a lightly floured surface. Press into a ball, cover with plastic wrap and refrigerate for 30 minutes.

Divide the dough into 3 portions. Roll out a portion, on a lightly floured surface, to fit the base of the tin. Divide another portion into thirds and roll each piece to line the side of the tin. Refrigerate the tin and the remaining portion of dough while preparing the filling.

Preheat the oven to 150°C (300°F/Gas 2). To make the filling, sift the flour, spices and ¼ teaspoon salt into a large bowl, then stir in the sugar, fruit, peel, almonds and zest. Mix well.

Lightly beat the eggs with the brandy, treacle and milk in a bowl, then mix into the fruit. The mixture should come together, but not be too wet.

Spoon the mixture into the pastry-lined tin and press into the base. The mixture will only come about three-quarters up the sides. Fold the pastry edges over the filling and brush the pastry with beaten egg. Roll out the remaining pastry, on a lightly floured surface, until large enough to cover the top. Trim to fit and press down firmly to seal. Prick the pastry top a few times with a fork. Brush with beaten egg and bake for 2–2½ hours. The top should be golden brown. If the pastry is over-browning, cover loosely with foil. Place the tin on a wire rack for 20 minutes to cool, then remove the side of the spring-form tin, and cool completely. When cold, store in an airtight container. Serve cut into wedges.

PREPARATION TIME: 45 MINUTES +   COOKING TIME: 2 HOURS 30 MINUTES

CRACKLE COOKIES

125 g (4½ oz) unsalted butter, softened
370 g (13 oz/2 cups) soft brown sugar
1 teaspoon vanilla essence
2 eggs
60 g (2¼ oz) dark chocolate, melted
80 ml (2¾ fl oz/⅓ cup) milk
340 g (12 oz/2¾ cups) plain (all-purpose) flour
2 tablespoons unsweetened cocoa powder
2 teaspoons baking powder
¼ teaspoon ground allspice
85 g (3 oz/⅔ cup) chopped pecans
icing (confectioners') sugar, to coat

MAKES ABOUT 60

Lightly grease two baking trays. Beat the butter, sugar and vanilla until light and creamy. Beat in the eggs, one at a time. Stir the chocolate and milk into the butter mixture. Sift the flour, cocoa, baking powder, allspice and a pinch of salt into the butter mixture and mix well. Stir the pecans through. Refrigerate for at least 3 hours, or overnight.

Preheat the oven to 180°C (350°F/Gas 4). Roll tablespoons of the mixture into balls and roll each in sifted icing sugar to coat. Place well apart on the trays to allow for spreading. Bake for 20–25 minutes, or until lightly browned and just firm. Leave on the trays for 3–4 minutes, then cool on a wire rack.

PREPARATION TIME: 20 MINUTES +   COOKING TIME: 25 MINUTES PER BATCH

DUNDEE CAKE

250 g (9 oz) unsalted butter, softened
230 g (8½ oz/1 cup) soft brown sugar
¼ teaspoon almond essence
2 teaspoons finely grated orange zest
2 teaspoons finely grated lemon zest
4 eggs, lightly beaten
250 g (9 oz/1⅔ cups) currants
320 g (11¼ oz/2 cups) sultanas (golden raisins)
80 g (2¾ oz/½ cup) raisins, chopped
60 g (2¼ oz/⅓ cup) mixed peel (mixed candied citrus peel)
100 g (3½ oz/⅔ cup) almonds, chopped
75 g (2½ oz/¾ cup) ground almonds
185 g (6½ oz/1½ cups) plain (all-purpose) flour
60 g (2¼ oz/½ cup) self-raising flour
½ teaspoon ground cinnamon
2 tablespoons whisky
100 g (3½ oz/⅔ cup) almonds, to decorate

MAKES 1

Preheat the oven to 150°C (300°F/Gas 2). Lightly grease a 20 cm (8 inch) round cake tin and line.

Beat the butter, sugar, essence and zests in a small bowl with electric beaters until light and fluffy. Add the eggs gradually, beating well after each addition. Transfer to a large bowl, stir in the dried fruits, mixed peel and chopped nuts, then the ground almonds, sifted flours, cinnamon and whisky. The batter should be just soft enough to drop from a spoon when shaken, so if it is too dry, add 1–2 tablespoons milk. Spread into the tin and smooth the surface. Wrap newspaper around the tin.

Arrange whole almonds on top of the cake in a spiral pattern. Place the tin on several layers of newspaper on the oven shelf. Bake for 2–2½ hours, or until a skewer comes out clean when inserted into centre of the cake. Cover the top with a sheet of baking paper, then cover tightly with foil and wrap in a thick tea towel (dish towel). Cool in the tin, then store in an airtight container for up to 3 months.

PREPARATION TIME: 35 MINUTES   COOKING TIME: 2 HOURS 30 MINUTES

BIEGLI

185 ml (6 fl oz/3/4 cup) milk, warmed
7 g (1/4 oz) sachet dried yeast
125 g (41/2 oz/1/2 cup) caster (superfine) sugar
500 g (1 lb 2 oz/4 cups) white strong flour
220 g (73/4 oz) butter, at room temperature
2 eggs, lightly beaten
1 teaspoon grated lemon zest
1 egg, lightly beaten, extra

WALNUT FILLING
400 g (14 oz/31/4 cups) walnuts
160 g (53/4 oz) sugar
75 g (21/2 oz/1/2 cup) currants
1 teaspoon finely grated lemon zest

MAKES 2

Pour 80 ml (23/4 fl oz/1/3 cup) warm milk into a small bowl. Sprinkle the yeast and a teaspoon of sugar over the surface, stir to dissolve and leave for 10 minutes, or until foamy.

Sift the flour into a large bowl and rub in the butter with your fingertips until the mixture resembles fine breadcrumbs. Make a well, add the yeast mixture, remaining milk and sugar, the eggs and lemon zest. Mix with a flat-bladed knife until the mixture comes together. Turn out onto a lightly floured work surface and knead lightly for 10 minutes. You may need to knead in up to 60 g (21/4 oz/1/2 cup) extra flour so the mixture is no longer sticky. Return to a clean bowl, cover with plastic wrap and leave in a warm place for 2 hours, or until doubled.

Meanwhile, for the filling, roughly chop the walnuts in a food processor, then transfer to a large bowl. Combine the sugar and 250 ml (9 fl oz/ 1 cup) water in a saucepan and stir over medium heat until the sugar has dissolved. Bring to the boil, reduce the heat and simmer for 10 minutes to reduce and thicken slightly. Remove from the heat and add to the ground walnuts. Stir in the currants and lemon zest and mix well. Set aside to cool.

Knock back the dough and knead on a lightly floured surface for 2–3 minutes. Divide into two and roll each portion into a rectangle about 22 x 36 cm (9 x 14 inches). Spread half the filling onto each, leaving a 2.5 cm (1 inch) border on all sides. Roll up from the short end to enclose the filling and place on a greased baking tray with the seam underneath. Cover with a tea towel (dish towel) and leave in a warm place for 11/2 hours, or until doubled in size.

Preheat the oven to 200°C (400°F/Gas 6). Brush the dough with extra beaten egg and prick the top in six places with a fork. Bake for 35–40 minutes, or until golden brown. Cover loosely with foil if over-browning. Cool on wire racks.

PREPARATION TIME: 25 MINUTES + RISING   COOKING TIME: 50 MINUTES

CERTOSINO

375 g (13 oz/3 cups) plain
(all-purpose) flour
1 teaspoon ground cinnamon
1/2 teaspoon freshly grated nutmeg
1 1/2 teaspoons bicarbonate of soda
(baking soda)
100 g (3 1/2 oz) unsalted butter
350 g (12 oz/1 cup) honey
205 g (7 1/4 oz/3/4 cup) apple sauce
110 g (3 3/4 oz/2/3 cup) sultanas (golden
raisins)
170 g (6 oz) blanched almonds,
coarsely chopped
50 g (1 3/4 oz/1/3 cup) pine nuts
75 g (2 1/2 oz) dark chocolate, chopped
185 g (6 1/2 oz/1 cup) mixed peel (mixed
candied citrus peel)
1 tablespoon rum
2 tablespoons apricot jam
icing (confectioners') sugar, to serve

MAKES 1

Preheat the oven to 160°C (315°F/Gas 2–3). Lightly grease a 23 cm (9 inch) springform cake tin and cover the base with baking paper.

Sift the flour, spices, bicarbonate of soda and 1/4 teaspoon salt into a large bowl. Make a well.

Combine the butter, honey and 2 tablespoons water in a saucepan over low heat, stirring until the butter has melted. Remove from the heat and pour into the well in the flour. Add the apple sauce, sultanas, nuts, chocolate, peel and rum and mix well. Spoon the mixture into the tin and bake for 1 1/4–1 1/2 hours, or until the cake is golden brown, feels firm and a skewer comes out clean when inserted into the centre. Cool in the tin for 20 minutes before turning out onto a wire cake rack to cool.

Stir the jam and 1 tablespoon water in a small saucepan over low heat until hot, then strain and brush all over the warm cake. Just before serving, dredge the top with icing sugar.

PREPARATION TIME: 30 MINUTES   COOKING TIME: 1 HOUR 30 MINUTES

SWEET PUFF PASTRY TWISTS

1 teaspoon cinnamon
2 tablespoons caster (superfine) sugar
2 sheets puff pastry
milk, for brushing

MAKES 24

Preheat the oven to 200°C (400°F/Gas 6). Stir the cinnamon through the caster sugar. Brush the puff pastry with milk and sprinkle the cinnamon sugar over the pastry.

Cut the pastry into 2 cm (3/4 inch) strips. Hold the ends of each strip and twist four times. Cover a baking tray with baking paper and bake a quarter of the strips for 5 minutes, or until golden, turning once. Repeat with the remaining twists.

PREPARATION TIME: 10 MINUTES +   COOKING TIME: 5 MINUTES PER BATCH

INDEX

INDEX